www.amagolf.co.kr

Address   Take Back   Half Swing   Swing Top

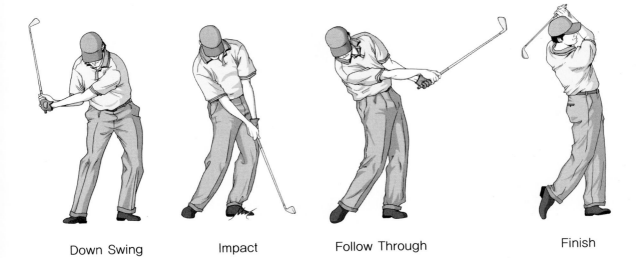

Down Swing   Impact   Follow Through   Finish

For the Amateur,
By the Amateur,
The Amateur Golf guide book

TURF TIPS

By Young Ho, Jung

Galim
Publisher

Turf Tips: For the amateur, by the amateur, the amateur golf guide book.
© 2007 by Young Ho, Jung. All rights reserved. Printed in the Republic of Korea. No part of this book may be used or reproduced in any manner whatsoever without written permission from Young Ho, Jung except in the case of brief quotations embodied in critical articles and reviews.

FIRST EDITION
First Printing, 2007

Galim Publisher
4F, Boowon Bldg., 57-71, Guui-dong, Gwangjin-gu, Seoul, Korea
www.galim.co.kr

ISBN 978-89-7895-258-3 03690

PROLOGUE

To some people there is nothing more enjoyable than playing golf. On the other hand, there are many golfers who find golf the most frustrating of sports, as they strive tirelessly to reduce their scores. There are numerous players who want to improve their skills, and these players take great efforts to continuously challenge themselves to get to the next par. Golf is a perfect sport for those who thrive on challenges. Golf is also an excellent activity for people who play it for pure enjoyment. I consider myself as one of the golf enthusiasts who seek to excel in the game. But at the same time, I try to enjoy it as much as possible.

We often hear that in the modern era everyone must play golf. It is said that golf is a great way to socialize with other people — a fun way to make friends and acquaintances. There are many reasons why golf is loved by so many people. Ever since I switched from tennis to golf as my sports activity of choice, I have been fanatical about it. Due to my love of the game, I have given a lot of thought about the following elements of becoming an effective golfer:

1. How one can understand the basics of the sport clearly and quickly.

2. How one can correctly follow what he or she has been taught.

3. How one can systematically learn the game of golf.

4. How one can understand the essence of the whole game in one glance?

These days, there is a constant demand of many people to obtain information about the game of golf easily, and to become a more effective player. In order to meet these demands, I have created a korean website (hhtp://www.amagolf.co.kr) as part of my efforts to share with many amateur golfers my life-long experiences and knowledge about golf. To further assist those who are motivated to learn the game of golf, and with the encouragement of my friends, I decided to write this book.

This book provides beginners with the basics of golf, ranging from technique, club selection, approach, and the execution of difficult shots. This book also provides information on appropriate golfing etiquette, common sense about selecting and handling clubs, golf stories contributed by golf amateurs including myself, and tips from my own personal experience to help novice golfers.

I sincerely hope that this book will be helpful to anyone who wants to learn to play golf better and more effectively. I want to thank my fellow players, and the employees of Karim Publishing Company for their support and assistance.

By Jung Young Ho

TABLE OF CONTENTS

CONTENTS

AMATEUR GOLF>>>

CONTENTS

CONTENTS

AMATEUR GOLF>>>

CONTENTS

AMATEUR GOLF>>>

CONTENTS

CONTENTS

CONTENTS

CONTENTS

CONTENTS

ARMATURE GOLF>>>

Part I

UNDERSTANDING AND PREPARING FOR GOLF

1. What is Golf?

When I visited a golf course for the first time as a beginner, my heart was pounding with expectation at the sight of the magnificent clubhouse. However, as excited as I was, I was in total confusion and didn't even know where to enter the golf course! Although I now feel at home on any golf course, at first I was quite at a loss at what to do.

Basically, a game of golf is played with a total of 14 golf clubs, and a golf ball measuring about 4.5cm in diameter. You have to get the golf ball into a hole of a diameter of 10.8cm within 3 to 5 strokes. The golf course consists of 18 holes and 72 par strokes in total: four par 5's, ten par 4's, and four par 3's. A par number refers to how many strokes it should take a player to get the ball into the hole. When it takes a player one more stroke than par, the player has scored a bogey; two more strokes, a double bogey; and three more strokes, a triple bogey. For a number of strokes more than three strokes over par, just add the number of additional strokes such as 4 or 5 to par to calculate your score. The total rounding distance of a golf course is about 6 to 7km, typically covering a total area of about 1 million square meters.

You should use a driver to tee off on the 14 par-4 and par-5 holes of 18. For the other four par-3 holes that are not long enough for a driver, you should use another club.

A par-5 hole typically requires three shots to get to the green, and two putts to get the ball into the hole. A par-4 hole requires two shots to get to the green, and two putts to get the ball into the hole. A par-3 hole requires one shot to get to the green, and two putts to get the ball into the hole. Therefore, when you play 72 strokes with 36 shots and 36 putts for the total 18 holes (consisting of 4 long, 10 middle and 4 short holes), your round of golf is referred to as "Even." When you finish a game with less than 72 strokes, your round is referred to as "Under."

For a par-5 hole, if you play four strokes to get the ball into the hole, you have scored a Birdi; three strokes, an Eagl; two strokes, an Albatros; and one stroke, a Hole in One. To calculate your score after the game, just add up all the differences between the number of strokes you made, and the par value of each hole. For example, if you played 68 strokes in total, your score is "4 Under (-4)."

In a PGA/LPGA game in the US, or a KPGA/KLPGA game in Korea, when a player records -3 (69 strokes) on the first day, -2 (70 strokes) on the second day, -4 (68 strokes) on the third day, and 0 (72 strokes) on the fourth day, their score is 279 strokes (-9). (The total par number of strokes is $72 \times 4 = 288$).

This is a very simple way to calculate a player's score. Even if you are an amateur golfer who began playing only recently, you will be able to explain this score to someone who doesn't know anything about golf.

2. How Should You Learn to Play Golf ?

When amateurs are interested in entering the amazing world of golf, they may be at a loss as to where, how, and from whom to learn how to play.

They may seek advice from their acquaintances, surf the Internet for information, or peek around indoor or outdoor golf training ranges. However, I believe that any beginner should start by studying the theories of golf. First of all, learn the basics of golf through a book, a video, TV, or the Internet. Ensure you understand the concept of swing, how to do a free swing and shoulder turning. Address the basics little by little. Then visit a driving range. By doing this, you will benefit greatly in the future.

When I taught my wife how to play golf, we used to go to a park early in the morning. I taught her about the swing path for 30 minutes after an hour of jogging. After three months, her swing was beautifully established, and her understanding of swing paths well developed. After that, she began to practice at driving ranges. At first, she practiced short swings, and then gradually increased her swing arc. Her progress was much faster than other beginners. She has been always thankful to me because this learning method helped her golf greatly.

★☆★ **Indoor Golf Range**

As there are few driving ranges, compared to the population who wants to learn to play golf, there are many indoor golf ranges, which are usually located in the basement or the second floor of a building. Here, golfers can learn the basics of golf swings in practice boxes. The distance is usually short — between 10 and 15 yards. You can usually learn the basic swings in about three months by practicing in one of these indoor golf ranges.

3. How To Play Golf Well?

The most important thing to playing golf well is to practice hard with a firm basis of theoretical knowledge. Think and be tactful when practicing golf. Select clubs that suit you. Find as good a coach as possible - and make sure you converse well with them.

Go to the golf course often. This is where a thinking game is required. Golf can become stressful if you try too hard to play well. Therefore, try to be a golfer who can enjoy playing, while studying and seeking the feeling of achievement. I will touch on the issue of how to enjoy golf later.

★☆★ **The history of Korean golf**

Golf was introduced to Koreans in 1900 by an Englishman who visited Korea as an adviser to the royal family of the Chosun Dynasty. He created a 6-hole course on the grounds of customs house at the beach in Wonsan. Later in 1919, an American created a 9-hole course in Hyochang Park in Seoul.

Korean golf started in earnest from 1920 when King Young Chin contributed 20,000 Won for the construction of an 18-hole golf course at the Seoul Children's Grand Park, the precursor to the Seoul Country Club.

The level of golf in Korea was displayed in 1941, when Yeon Duk Choon, an unknown Korean golfer, won the Japan Open with 290 shots.

In 1954, after the Korean War, a par 72-hole course opened at the Children's Grand Park, which marked the gradual development of golf in Korea. The Seoul Country Club that was in the Children's Grand Park was later moved to Wondang in Goyangshi, Gyeongido.

4. Selecting the Right Club

Typically, you will buy your clubs based on the recommendations of your acquaintances or professional players at golf shops.

Above all, you need to base your club selection on club length. The length of the clubs you choose must be suitable for your body shape, shaft strength, weight of the club, and swing weight. You will also want to consider brand and price. The best choice is the one that offers great performance with a reasonable price tag.

When you are buying clubs for the first time, second-hand irons with good performance will suffice. However, it is always better to buy a new driver. You also need a good putter that feels just right for you. After all, you will eventually have to replace your clubs. You will be better able to select the perfect clubs after you have played a while.

Fairway woods don't have to bear the name of a famous brand. These days, there are many companies who produce fine clubs at reasonable prices. In addition, you will also need a golf bag, a clothing bag, T-shirts, gloves, golf shoes, golf stockings, golf clothes, and a hat. Now you are ready for the golf course.

Tidbits of Information

★☆★ **The history of golf clubs**

Although there are no accurate records, it seems that in the beginning, wooden shafts were used as clubs. Later, English longbow craftsmen produced the first technical clubs as a side job. Historical records suggest a master club-maker once exclusively made clubs for the royal family in 1618, during the days of King James the First. At the time, golf was played with just one or two clubs. It was around 1934 that carrying many clubs became fashionable. By this stage, golf was being played with as many as 20 clubs. Many players complained that too many golf clubs were distorting the game. As a result, golfers limited the number of clubs to 14 as a rule for official games. This rule continues to this day.

| 1 Driver | 3 Woods | 9 Irons | 1 Putter |

Players carry 14 clubs on average. The above is the standard assortment, but this changes depending on the individual preferences of the player.

5. A Training Program for Amateurs (180-Day Program)

1) With the help of your acquaintances, obtain clubs that best fit your physique.

2) Study and practice your swing with out balls for 15 to 20 days in a park or at a driving range.

    a. Do video analysis.

    b. Practice your swings paying attention to your center of axis and circular movements.

3) Practice short swings for 3 days and putting for 3 days still without balls.

4) Hit balls with the irons. Repeat the following twice for 84 days in total:

    a. Short swing: 5 days   b. 1/4 swing: 7 days

    c. 1/2 swing: 10 days   d. 3/4 swing: 10 days   e. Full swing: 10 days

-------------------------------------- 90 Days --------------------------------------

5) Practice swings with woods (No balls):

    a. Driver (practice rhythm and tempo): 4 days

    b. No. 3, 4, 5, and 7 wooden clubs (practice rhythm and tempo): 4 days

6) Hit balls with the woods:

    a. Driver: 10 days

    b. No. 3, 4, 5, and 7 woods: 10 days

7) Hit balls with the driver and irons:

1 day practice	60 days
Short swing (iron) 20% Half swing (iron) 20% Full swing (driver) 40% Full swing (iron) 20%	Repeat practices

8) Hit balls with the driver and irons:

Driver: 5 days

Irons # 7&5: 5 days

Practice for approximately 6 months

9) Spend a day to learn the basics of golf courses, the game management, and etiquette on the course.

10) Study a simple description of the rules for a day

--- 180 days ---

11) Course

Training programs for amateur golfers may vary depending on the individual's capabilities. If you get through the training program, you will be able to get a real taste for golf. You can even become a single digit-handicap player after one year. Enjoy the game of golf to the fullest!

Part 2.

FUNDAMENTALS

All the information that follows in this manual is written for right-handed players. For left-handed players, all you need to do is reverse the information given. For example, when I say to grip the club with your left hand, left-handers will need to use their right hand.

1. Grip

Grip is an essential part of the game - like fastening the first button on a jacket. Your grip will contribute greatly to the development of your golf game. A golfer's grip is like the golf is face. It must be steady and correctly shaped to ensure the best start to a golfing career.

There are three types of grips that are based on the way you hold a club with your fingers. Another three types relate to the direction of the back of your hand.

1) Three ways to hold the club with your fingers

① Interlocking Grip

This is suitable for females and children with small hands, or physically weak males. Incidentally, Jack Nicklaus uses this grip.

② Overlapping Grip

This is the most widely used grip. Strong people with powerful hands, would-be professional players, professional players, and most amateurs prefer this grip.

③ Baseball Grip

This grip is suitable for Asians, women with small hands, and children who are not very strong. It is not a widely used grip, but I recommend it for female players. It is also good for those with weaker hands.

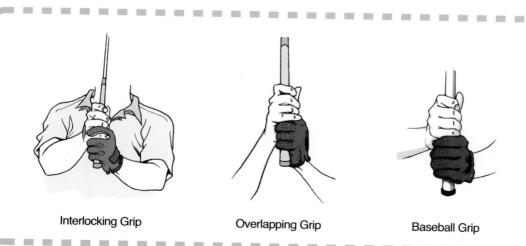

| Interlocking Grip | Overlapping Grip | Baseball Grip |

2) Three types of grips based on direction

① Square Grip

This grip, in which your hands face each other, is the most preferred grip for hitting a straight ball.

② Strong Grip

This is a kind of hook grip. Turn your left hand until you can see about three knuckles of the back of your left hand. Turn your right hand to the right slightly more than you would in a square grip. This grip is often used for a hook ball or for strong impact.

③ Weak Grip

This is a kind of slice grip. Turn your left hand until you can see about two knuckles of the back of your left hand. Turn your right hand far to the left. This grip is mostly used for slice balls. Other than professionals and those for whom it has become a habit, this grip is not widely used.

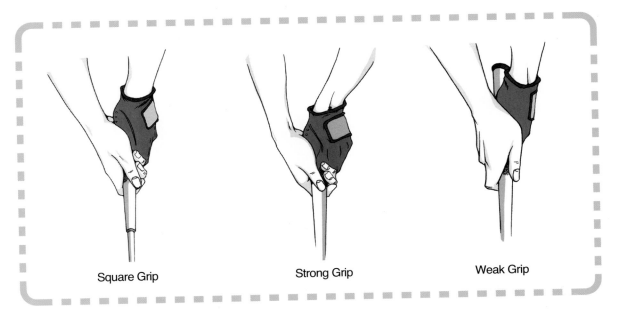

Square Grip   Strong Grip   Weak Grip

3) How to make a grip

Slowly but firmly wrap the handle of a club with last three fingers of your left hand, starting with the little finger.

Gently place your thumb and index finger on the club. Hold your thumb, little, and index fingers as shown in the figure below. Hold your other fingers as shown in the figure. You should keep practicing to have a grip as good as the one in the figure.

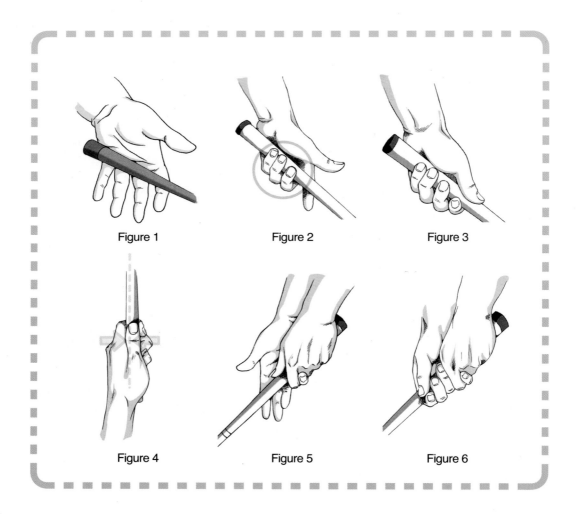

Figure 1   Figure 2   Figure 3

Figure 4   Figure 5   Figure 6

4) Precautions and checkpoints for grip

Firstly, the grip must be firm without any gaps between your hands, as if you are holding your lover in your arms···.

Secondly, the grip should not be too loose, and the hands must be kept firm at any point during a swing, especially at the top and finish of the swing.

Thirdly, never hold your right hand loosely for smother swings.

Fourthly, always remember that the right grip can be established only when you make it a habit to hold the club firmly, and relax the rest of your body at the same time.

Fifthly, in any type of grip, both hands must be placed together in good, solid formation. You should closely watch and imitate the grips of professionals. There are grip-practicing devices at golf shops that can be used to help establish a sound grip.

Finally, pay attention to the formation of a V-shape between your thumb and index fingers.

2. Stance

1) Stance and the position of the ball

Stance is the key to whether or not your body can maintain balance during the circular movement of a swing. In other words, you need a firm stance to balance the center of your body's axis during left and right back swings or during follow through. In general, a golfer's stance depends on their shoulder width and the club they are using.

I recommend that amateur golfers do not think too hard about their stance. The width

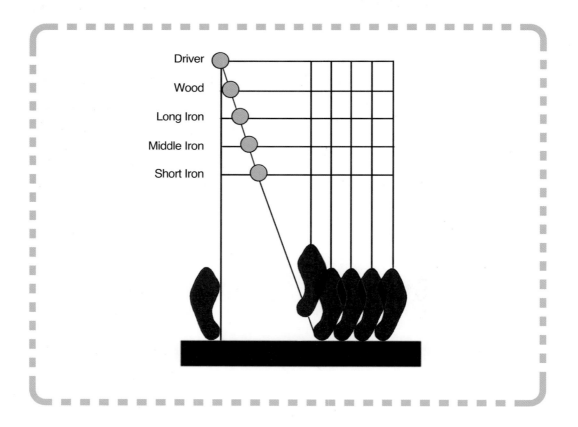

between your feet and the position of the ball with respect to your body are complex issues that many beginners can be confused by. Here are some tips that I usually give:

① For a driver, your stance may be as wide as, or wider than, your shoulder width. Align the heel of your left foot with the ball and make a closed stance.

② For woods, move the ball a little further to the right than for a driver. Having said that, do not be too concerned with the position of the ball. The position of the ball and your stance will vary slightly. Maintaining a firm position on the ground is more important.

③ For irons, always place your feet equal distance from the ball. Keep the width between your feet narrower than your shoulder length. Your stance should be square, but it can also be open or closed.

④ For an approach, put the ball a little to the right of center between your feet. However, your stance should be open. Keep the width between your feet narrow.

As shown in the figure, have the ball near your left foot for a driver, woods, or long irons. For irons, have the ball centered between your feet. For short irons, a slightly open stance is better.

2) Types of stance

Stance refers to the way you position your feet and the width between them.

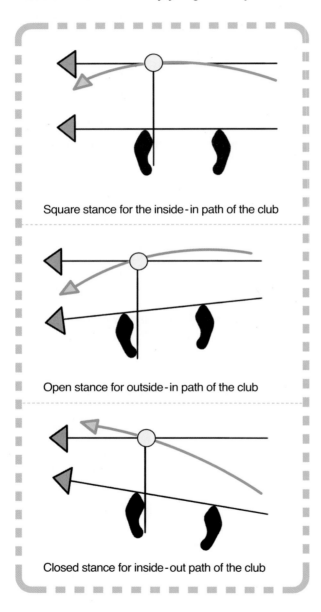

Square stance for the inside-in path of the club

Open stance for outside-in path of the club

Closed stance for inside-out path of the club

① **Square Stance**

The positions of your feet and the ball are parallel. The swing path will be inside-in for a straight shot.

② **Open Stance**

Your right foot is slightly further away from the ball than your left foot. The swing path will be outside-in for a slice shot.

③ **Closed Stance**

Your left foot is a little further away from the ball than your right foot. The swing path is inside-out for a hook shot.

3) Stance by body shape

For a driver, the heel of your left foot should be on a straight line with the ball. For # 3, 4, and 5 woods, move your right foot little by little to the left. For long irons, your stance should be similar to wood # 5, and for middle irons (# 5, 6, 7), the ball should be placed equal distance from each foot.

For short irons, the ball may be equal distance from each foot, or slightly to the right. The most important point for address and stance is to maintain the center of your body's gravity at the front of your feet in a comfortable way. The width between your feet must be appropriate to your body shape.

For example, if you are tall, a narrow stance may cause the axis of swing to sway. If you are rather short or fat, too wide a stance may cause difficulties in shifting your weight to swing. Therefore, you should adjust your stance appropriately for your body shape and your strength.

In some cases, such as when you have not fully recovered from "the night before," your stance should be slightly wider than usual to maintain balance!

The most natural posture would be to stand straight, push your hip out backwards like a duck, and bend your knees slightly. In this posture, your arms will naturally drop down. In this state, hold the club and align your feet with the width of your shoulders. Ensure that the weight of your body is evenly spread over the front and the rear of the soles of your feet.

3. Address

The key point to the address is that you have a comfortable and stable posture. Firstly, align your feet with the width of your shoulder, push your hip slightly backwards like a duck, keeping your backbone and head straight.

Now, bend your knees slightly and drop your arms down naturally. Take the club in your left hand. Your left hand should be approximately one or two fists away from your left thigh. Then, gently place your right hand on the club. Now your right shoulder will be one fist lower than your left shoulder. Once you are in this position, turn your whole body 10° to the righ—your left shoulder will be slightly closed. This is the best address pose.

The steps to the address pose

Push your hip backwards like a duck, and bend your knees slightly.

1) Checkpoints for address

① Are your backbone and head arched?

② Do you feel that the center of your body's gravity is firmly supported on the soles of your feet even when you move your body forwards, backwards, to the right, and to the left?

③ Are your shoulders raised or too tense while gripping the club?

④ Have you decided on the direction of the ball?

⑤ Is your pose comfortable and stable?

⑥ Is the distance between your hands and your body appropriate?

    - For driver: two fists

    - For irons: one and a half fists

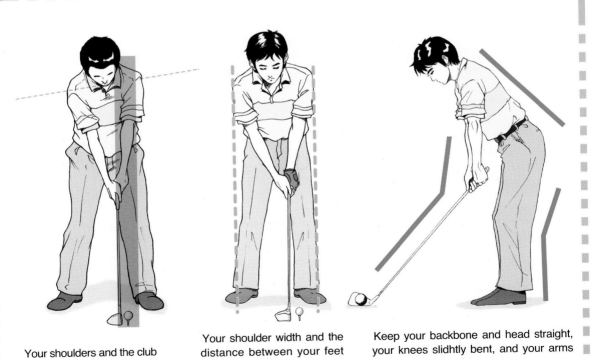

Your shoulders and the club must be on a straight line.

Your shoulder width and the distance between your feet must be equal.

Keep your backbone and head straight, your knees slidhtly bent, and your arms naturally hanging down.

4. Back Swing Start

When your stance and address are established, you can start your swing. The start of a swing is the back swing. As the saying goes, "Well begun is half done." The start of your swing must be natural, so that the path to the top of the back swing will be smooth. Your back swing should be smooth, effortless, and natural. Most amateurs find it very difficult. So, you need to practice the following :

① Swing the club left and right like a pendulum.
② Waggle the club with your wrists relaxed.
③ Start your swing after touching the ground with your club, or by pressing the club slightly to the left.

You need to make every effort to create a smooth back swing. When you begin your back swing, your left shoulder, left arm, and the club, must move in one flowing, straight movement. You should continue to push the club for over 10 inches past your bottom, past your waist, and to the top of the arc in one single movement.

If your back swing is too slow, the rhythm will be broken, and your hands and shoulders will become tense. This makes the down swing difficult. The support of your right lower body should not loosen, and your left hip should not follow in.

★☆★ **Waggle**

This is the preliminary movement before the back swing, in which you move the club head with short, quick motions over the ball. The purpose of the waggle is to focus your mind and relax your muscles.

Start the back swing after confirming the support of your right foot.

Make the back swing while holding your wrists steady, as if your shoulder and the club are one piece.

★ ☆ ★ The history of the golf ball

The first golf balls were made of feathers. Feathers were stuffed in an animal skin bag, which was then stitched up. However, its performance was changeable with the weather. When it was wet and rainy, the feather ball's flying distance diminished. As it was light, its flight was also strongly affected by the wind.

Later in 1844, "gutta percha" balls were introduced. They were made from solidified sap. These balls marked the beginning of mass production of golf balls. After that, two-piece balls were developed. These were made with wound elastic strings inside the ball. Following that, three-piece balls, and later, titan balls (with titanium powder stuffed inside) were introduced.

The dimples on the surface of golf balls were developed by chance. It was discovered that balls with bruises flew further. After the fact was proven, golf balls with about 300 to 500 dimples were introduced.

5. Half Swing

There is no need to describe the half swing separately, but there are a few precautions to be aware of.

First of all, when your left hand is stretched out to waist level, the handle of the club must be directed towards the target, and the face of the club must be directed forwards. Furthermore, the cocking of your wrists should be formed naturally, but directed to the thumb of your left hand. Your left shoulder sit under your chin, and the club head must be stretched as far as possible from your body.

You must remember that the half back swing and the half follow through must be symmetrical. Therefore, practicing left and right half swings while maintaining your head at the center of the stroke is more important than any other exercise.

Natural cocking
after a half swing

6. Swing Top

The swing top is the position that you reach by pushing your shoulder in slightly further than where it is in a half swing. The rhythm and tempo of your back swing will only be harmonized when your swing moves up naturally.

To give a more detailed description, the swing top is where the club moves up backwards, by the rebound of the forward and backward movements, and then stops while you practice the half swing by rotating your shoulders.

In other words, the ideal swing top is determined by the rebound. It can also be described as the state in which the club cannot be moved back any further, because the cocking of your left wrist cannot turn over backwards, with the firm support of the thumb of your left hand.

If your back swing goes further backward from this point, it is because you made an incorrect body movement, such as your wrist bending inside, or your body swaying with your hip following in, or the left part of your waist stretched.

> ★☆★ **Sway**
> Moving the centerline of your body to the left, right, up, or down during a swing.

If you have practiced your grip, stance, address, back swing, half swing, and swing top, half of your swing is completed. Let's summarize what we have learned so far :

① Never use your wrists during a back swing, but push the club as if your shoulder and the club are part of one body.

② Keep the club head low so that it will travel 10 to 15 inches, almost touching the ground.

③ Keep the club head from leaving the right line of your body to the front or rear during the half swing.

④ Are your hands tense because the swing rhythm is broken during the back swing? You should make a consistent one-piece swing.

⑤ Pay attention while moving to the swing top, so that your left hip will not follow too far, and the left part of your waist is stretched.

⑥ Is your weight loaded on your right foot?

Is the angle of your right knee maintaining the angle during the address?

⑦ Is the cocking naturally formed? In other words, is your left thumb supporting the club well?

⑧ Now, are you ready to move the club down?

The movement down from the swing top should start at the right turning point that is neither too early nor too late. In other words, wait one tempo before moving down if you feel it's too early. Move down directly from the swing top if you feel it's too late.

⑨ Compared to females and juniors whose shoulders are usually more flexible, some males with more rigid bodies need practice making good shoulder turns. However, females and juniors should take special care not to loosen their wrists during a down swing due to their relative lack of strength.

★☆★ **Tackling a par-3 hole**

Get on to the green with the tee shot and play one or two putts. There are four par-3 holes among the 18 holes.

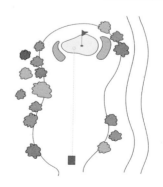

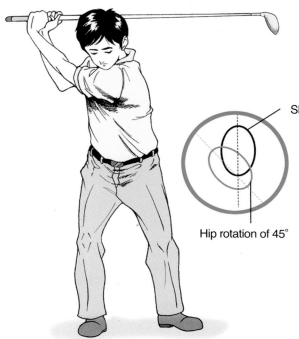

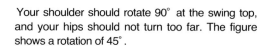

Shoulder rotation of 90°

Hip rotation of 45°

Your shoulder should rotate 90° at the swing top, and your hips should not turn too far. The figure shows a rotation of 45°.

From the swing top, your right elbow should face the ground, and the angle between your body and your arm should be about 80 ~ 90°.

7. Down Swing

It is not difficult to swing the club down from the top.

However, you should swing your club down by your shoulder, without releasing the cock of the wrist. If cocking of the club is released, you must remember when it was released and what the down path of the club was. While you move your weight to the left and throw your club towards the ball, you must support the left side of your body well. Since this whole process happens in an instant, you must focus.

Therefore, the down swing is truly the enemy of amateur golfers. All errors occur in this movement. We must learn not to be caught in a trap here.

① Be aware of the timing of your movement down from the swing top.

② Swing down effortlessly and fluidly. In other words, pull down the swing top pose intact, without releasing the cocking by the turn of your shoulder.

③ When the club moves down to your waist, release your right elbow. Release your wrist as late as possible.

④ Even if the weight of your lower body moves to the left, your head should not move.

⑤ In the same manner as your shoulder and arm form a triangle during the back swing, your right and left arms and wrist cocking should not change when swinging down from the top. In order to do this, the down movement must be led by the turn of your shoulder. Furthermore, your right foot should give way to the outside so that your right arm can move inside. Your weight should shift naturally to the left, while your right arm is spread at waist level. The triangular pose of your arms will return to the original form of the address until impact.

⑥ The most difficult thing is to prevent your body from following your arms during the back swing and the down swing. In other words, in the same manner as your weight is shifted

Making a down swing while keeping the cocking at the swing top, and releasing it just before impact

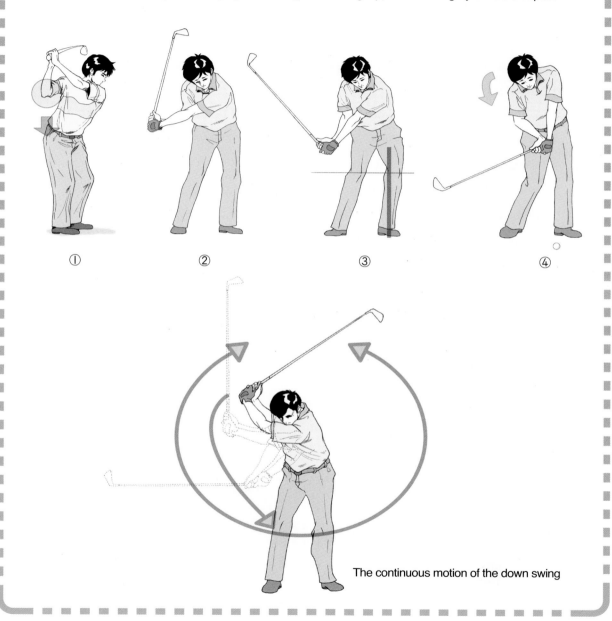

① ② ③ ④

The continuous motion of the down swing

without the lower body being pushed during the back swing right up until the swing top, so too should your weight be shifted without your lower body being pushed during the down swing until the impact. It is not an overstatement to say that this is everything in golf. The path of the down swing must be inside-out. Your wrist should come down without the cocking released. Your head and body should not sway left and right or up and down.

⑦ To express this simply, you should not move your head up, and your head and shoulders should not move in front of your club. In other words, impact with the ball should be made while keeping your head and body at the back. This habit of a sound down swing must be mastered by repeated practice.

Practice the movement from the back swing top to the down swing in front of a mirror about 50 times a day for a month. Can you make your down swing naturally, with the support of your lower body and without the cocking being released? You should practice this until you can answer, "Yes"

★ ☆ ★ **Playing for a par - 4 hole:**

After the tee shot and the second shot, make one or two putts into the hole.

There are 10 par -4 holes out of 18 holes.

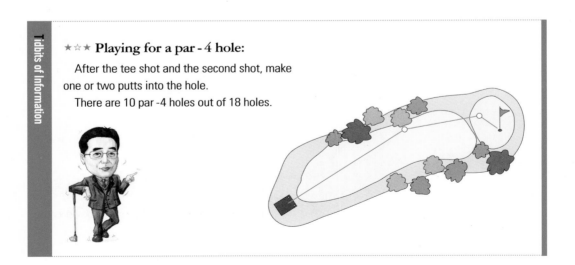

8. Impact

A correct down swing makes for correct impact.

In other words, the head of your club must be at a right angle to the ball, within the path, to make correct impact. The club must be on the inside path to be at a right angle to the ball at the impact point, so that the ball flies straight and with power.

Checkpoints for Impact :

① Do not try to hit the ball. Instead, have a sense of hitting through it. It is as if the club head follows the ball after hitting it.

② Make a triangle with your shoulders and arms. Maintain a sense of stretching your arms during impact.

③ Have a sense of holding the ball while hitting it during impact.

④ Always keep your head at the back of the ball.

⑤ There is no impact without the support of your left body.

⑥ Impact is weak if the arms extend out too far from the torso.

⑦ Practice free down swings a lot with the support of your lower body.

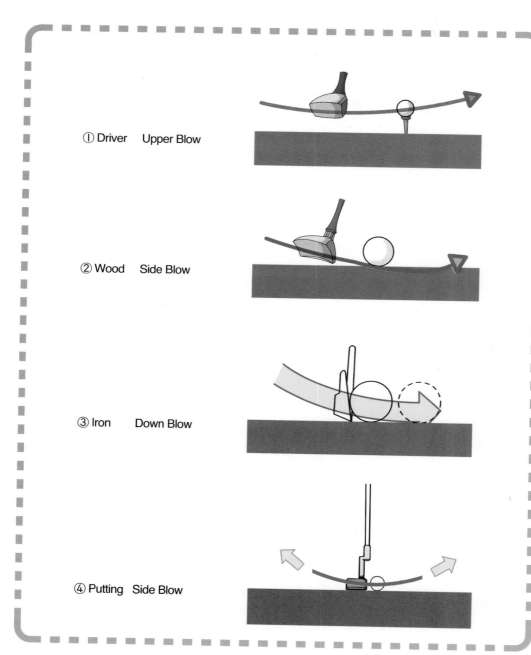

① Driver   Upper Blow

② Wood   Side Blow

③ Iron   Down Blow

④ Putting Side Blow

The power of impact depends on the angle of your club. Always try to make square impact.

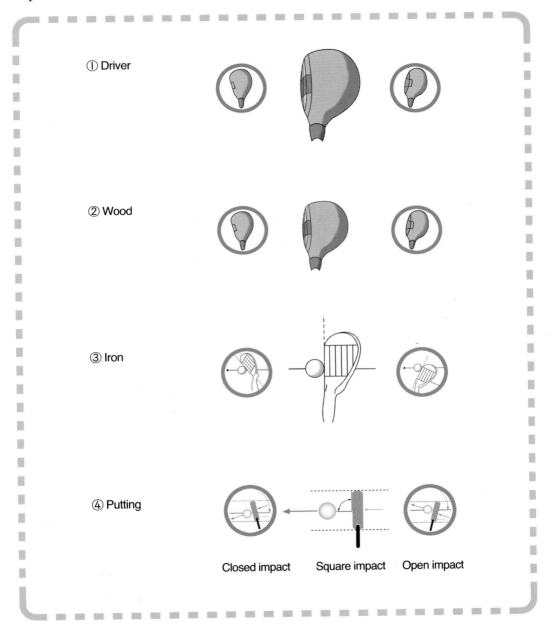

① Driver

② Wood

③ Iron

④ Putting

Closed impact   Square impact   Open impact

9. Follow Through & Finish

When impact is well executed, the follow through should be naturally good. At impact, the ball should be at a right angle to the club head, and you should have the feeling that the ball is moving together with the head.

At this time, your right shoulder must move under your chin, which is symmetrical to your left shoulder moving under your chin while your left arm is stretched during the back swing.

As your weight shifts in this way, your right arm follows the direction of the ball together with your club, which creates a long follow through. After this, the follow through is completed by the turn of your body and shoulders.

You may often feel that your finish on the golf course is not as fluid as it seems at the driving range.

Why is this so? The reason is that at the driving range, you often just try to hit the ball. If you hit the ball, there can be no follow through because your swing ends at the point of impact. On the wide, open field, your concentration is naturally hampered. Amateur golfers in the beginning of their golfing careers invariably feel confused on the golf course.

In such a state of mind, they can play an entire 18-hole round without knowing when the club was raised and lowered during the back swing and down swing! A stable and natural finish can be made only when the follow through is well done, and body weight is shifted naturally.

If you ensure you do not allow your body to turn too fast or follow your arms, and that your weight does not shift incorrectly, your finish will be sound.

To explain this geometrically, the follow through is symmetrical to half of the back swing, and the top of back swing is symmetrical to the finish.

There are a few precautions to be aware of :

① You should support your left axis.

② Your head should remain at the back of the ball.

③ Your right shoulder should turn under your chin.

④ For the follow through, your weight should shift and your arms should be stretched straight, following the ball with the power of impact.

⑤ Your pose should be stable after finishing your follow through.

Your body and arms should move together in sync. Your left arm should move in unison with your torso during the follow through. If your head keeps its position, your right arm will not separate from the body.

High finish with the right arm stretched straight.

Follow through

The sole of your left foot should 'stick' to the ground to support your weight.

The sole of your foot should stand straight and the angle between your left arm and body should be 90°, symmetrical to the back swing.

Part 3.

GOLF TECHNIQUES

1. Cocking

Cocking is naturally formed from the waist and up during the back swing. At the swing top, the cock is formed in the direction of your thumb, which is the swing top.

If the cock's direction is not towards the thumb but to the back or palm of your hand, the club's face will point to a wrong direction. Which makes it difficult to hit the ball straight.

By waiting to release the cock right before impact, you will have power in your impact, and your follow through will follow the ball. This will make it easier to hit the ball straight. Amateur golfers should not try too hard to form a perfect cock. They should instead try to form it naturally.

The cock of your wrist is a preliminary action to add power to the impact. It is the driving force of the impact.

A correct cocking, where the back of the left hand and arm are straight

An incorrect cocking, where the wrist of the left hand is bent too far towards the ground

An incorrect cocking, where the wrist of the left hand is bent too far forwards

Always bear in mind that you should release the cock at the point of impact, and the wrist of your left hand should not be bent.

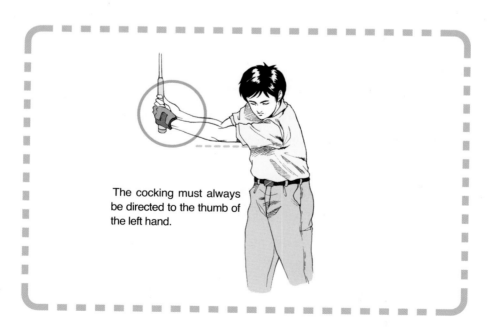

The cocking must always be directed to the thumb of the left hand.

2. Shoulder Turn

From the start of the back swing, your shoulder should turn slowly over 90°, so that you could see your shoulder in the mirror. Your hip should turn a half of your shoulder's turn (45°). At this point, you should keep your left hip from being pushed to the right.

Furthermore, your shoulders will turn more easily if you turn it while your right knee stays bent and your right leg is holding most of the tension. Your twisted shoulder should not hide your chin but come under it. During this back swing, all parts of your body, including the knee, hip, waist, and shoulder, should turn in parallel to the ground.

When the shoulder turn is formed correctly, the down swing becomes easier and impact is more powerful.

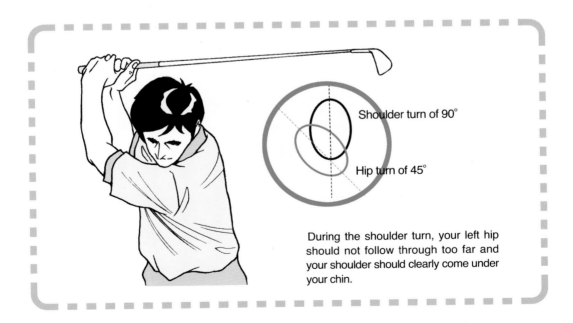

Shoulder turn of 90°

Hip turn of 45°

During the shoulder turn, your left hip should not follow through too far and your shoulder should clearly come under your chin.

3. Shift of Weight

There are three axes : center, right and left. During the back swing, your right knee should support the weight of the left side of your body. Your center of gravity should be shifted to the right by at least 80%. At the swing top, you should prepare to shift your weight that was completely shifted to the right side of your body to the left again.

Upon impact, your weight is shifted more to the left by 60:40 as at the address. At the follow through, all the weight of the right side of your body is shifted to the left, and your right thigh should stick to your left thigh. The shifting of weight should be effected as much as the axis of your body can support. Furthermore, it is important that this weight shift should be made within the fixed axes of right and left. Therefore, you need to take special care to prevent your body from swaying during the weight shift. In other words, you should keep your body from wobbling up and down or left and right while shifting weight from left to right.

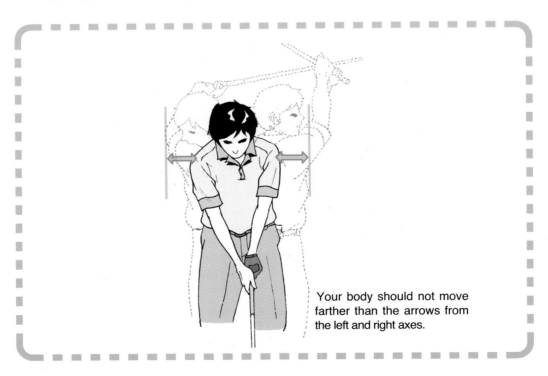

Your body should not move farther than the arrows from the left and right axes.

4. Support of the Lower Body

To maintain solid balance of your lower body, your setup pose must be firm. The right axis during the back swing, the center axis during impact, and the left axis during follow through should not sway, and should be supported by your knees. The stronger the support and the faster the swing, the further the distance you can achieve.

Most important is the support of your left hip during the back swing. If your left hip follows in, your waist will be straightened, the twist of the waist is lost, and your body sways. Therefore, you should prevent your left hip from being pushed during the back swing. The second condition for the support of your lower body is that your supporting side knee should never be straightened.

The best thing you can do is to make a shoulder turn of 90° during the back swing while your body below the waist does not move. Moreover, the axis of your head should not follow the swing—this also helps to support your lower body.

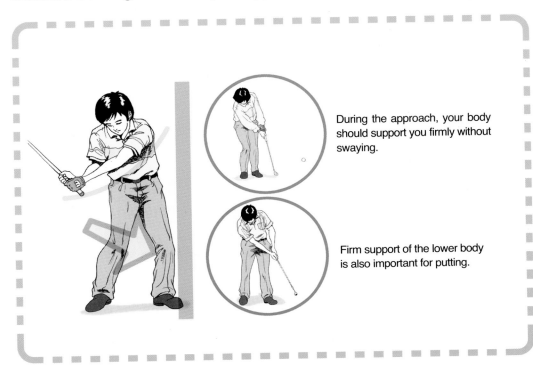

During the approach, your body should support you firmly without swaying.

Firm support of the lower body is also important for putting.

5. Side-to-Side Movement

Side-to-side movement refers to the sway phenomenon where the axis breaks down. Side-to-side movement should always be parallel to the ground, and you should always keep your hip following the inside during the back swing.

The straightening of your waist and knees during the back swing are the changes of side-to-side movement. If you pay attention to these things, a slight side-to-side movement is not a big problem. In any case, you should never move beyond the borderlines of the axis. Some side-to-side movement is OK, as long as it is within the confines of the axis.

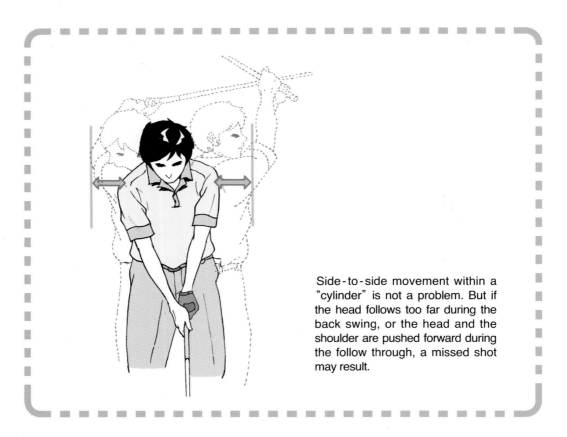

Side-to-side movement within a "cylinder" is not a problem. But if the head follows too far during the back swing, or the head and the shoulder are pushed forward during the follow through, a missed shot may result.

6. Up and Down Movement

The worst habit in golf is up and down movement. In particular, if your waist and knees are straightened during the back swing, you will not be able to turn your shoulder. If the shoulder turn is not formed, the down swing is made with only your arms. Power in the impact will be lost. Moving your head up is also a bad habit. If there is no up and down movement, your golf will almost be perfect.

In particular, when you straighten up during the back swing, your body will drop during down swing. This is the main cause of a sliced shot. Most amateurs get caught in this trap. By paying attention to maintaining the angle of your knees, maintaining your strength, and keeping your head up, your shot will be good.

You should bend your knees slightly.

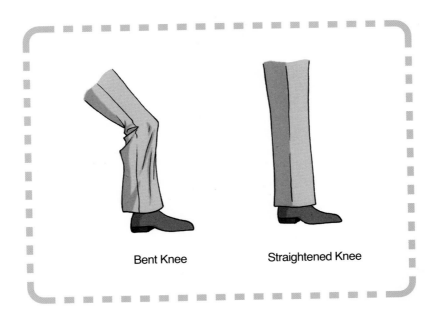

Bent Knee   Straightened Knee

Your knees should not be too straight or bent, and the angle of the knees at the address should not change during a swing.

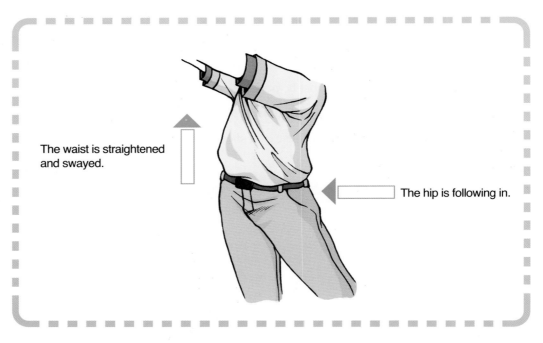

The waist is straightened and swayed.

The hip is following in.

★☆★ Playing a par-5 hole

After the tee shot, the second shot, and the third shot, make one or two putts.

There are 4 par-5 holes in an 18-hole course.

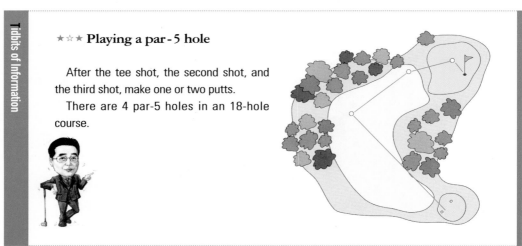

7. Forming a V with Hands and Forearm

The triangle made with your shoulders and arms should stay the same from the start of the back swing to the follow through. The swing is powered by the turn of your shoulder.

The extent to which your shoulders and arms move together directly affects the direction and impact of your stroke. It also helps maintain balance in your swing. Always bear in mind that in the impact zone, your shoulders and arms should move together.

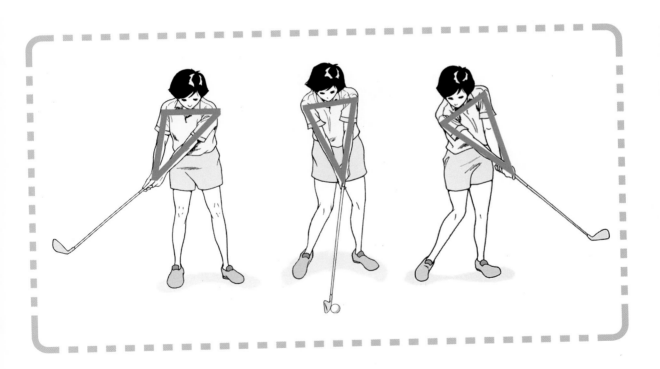

8. Parallel Movement of Hands

The grip of your hands should keep a distance of two fists from your thigh while moving from the address to the back swing, and moving back from the back swing. In other words, your hands should move in parallel with the front of your body, and maintain the same distance.

If your arms and body are too far from each other, you are effectively just swinging your arms without any power or direction. If this is a problem for you, you should practice your half swing with a towel under your arms. The back swing and the follow through should be made with your arms and body not too far apart.

Practice your swing with a towel under your arms. If your chest and arms do not move too far apart, the towel will not fall.

9. Down Swing: Natural Falling of Hands

How do you perform a down swing? How do you collect your mind to begin the down swing after a restless back swing? This is a very important issue on which there are many different theories.

In my opinion, the best method is to move your arms down as you keep the same arm and shoulder angles with a feel of slightly pulling your left shoulder.

As you should form a triangle at the start of the back swing, maintain the pose at the top during the down swing, starting with the turn of your shoulder. This way, your club will fall easily without your effort.

The most common theory dictates that the down swing should start by the lead of the lower body: starting from the foot, the hip, and then the shoulder. A more recent theory suggests that since the lower body will lead on its own by the mere thought of the down swing from the top, you simply need to throw down the club.

However, if an amateur golfer tries to follow such advice, only his arm will swing. If the cock is released too early, he will be in trouble. It is a well-known fact that the cock should not be released until just before impact, in order to create speed at impact. As you can see from the centrifugal force, when you turn a weight with a string attached to it, the weight should follow the movement. You may think of the shoulder axis as the center and the club head as the weight.

It is important to think of hitting the ball with the lead of the lower body. But it is more beneficial for amateurs not to try to move the lower body too much. If weight is shifted appropriately, your body will move naturally.

If your shoulder maintains the top swing pose during the down swing, the down swing can be made without releasing the cocking of the wrists.

10. Holding for a Moment during Impact

If your body and head move forward of the ball upon impact, you will not feel the clear impact. However, if the club passes the ball while your head and body are behind the ball, you can feel the impact clearly.

At the moment when the club hits the ball, you should feel as if the club hits and then passes the ball. In other words, you should feel as if the club rests for a moment and you are hitting the ball while holding it. Amateurs need to develop the right feel during the impact.

Do not miss the moment of impact. Seize the moment.

11. Following through the Ball with Your Club

In following through, you should feel as if the ball is attached to the head of the club, and moving towards the target.

When the ball meets the club at a right angle, and the follow through after impact is executed well, you will feel the sensation of the ball being attached to the club as it flies.

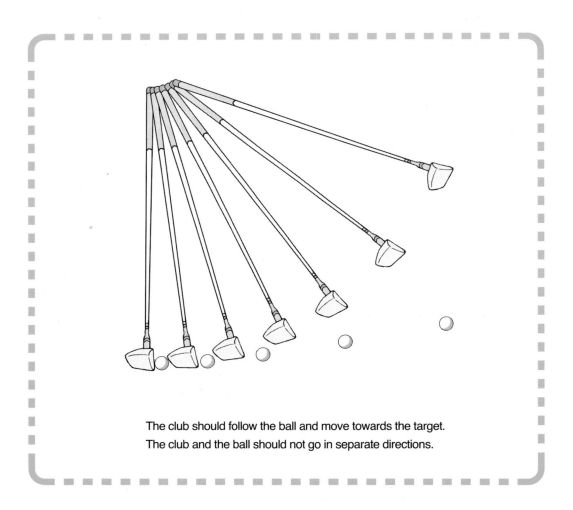

The club should follow the ball and move towards the target.
The club and the ball should not go in separate directions.

12. The Sensation You Should Get While Swinging

Amateurs can enjoy this sensation more than professional golfers. The sensation of a correct swing after making so many poor swings is as satisfying a feeling as any!

"This is it!" Pros may enjoy this less than amateurs—when everything goes smoothly, the 'right' shot doesn't stand out as much. To fully feel and appreciate the sensation of a correct swing, you need to have many ups and downs—just like life itself. The wider the gap between joy and sorrow, the more fully may we experience the joy. For example, a stock price hitting the upper limit gives us joy today, but the same stock hitting the lower limit tomorrow sends us to the depths of despair. This is just like a graph of our lives.

These feelings are identical for beginning golfers. I have always thought of golf in this way: Golf is the game of humanity. Sometimes you win. Sometimes you lose. From Royalty to servant, from the President of a nation to the common man on the street, we all have our ups and downs. And so too, on the golf course, do we all have our ups and downs.

Similarly, every golfer shares the same emotions when they play golf. Therefore, it is only natural that everybody loves golf. It is the sport that unifies us as human beings.

I talk about conceptual feelings, but in essence what I'm trying to address are the sensations you feel when you swing a golf club.

In the process of learning golf, every amateur golfer has a sense of his/her own way. The best way to feel the sense of all swings is to practice free swings.

During free putting, we can swing like a pendulum with only our shoulders and without shaking our wrists, and we can feel the support of our legs. Try to keep the sense of free swinging in mind as long as possible when you face a stroke.

These are a few checkpoints about what you feel, and what you should feel during a putt:

① The sense that you can do the stroke well when you support your left foot firmly on the ground.

② You putt better when you have a stable stance, with the entire soles of your feet stepping on the ground as if driving in a stake.

③ You putt better when the putter follows the ball farther to the hole after impact.

④ You putt better when you push the putter up and forward.

⑤ You putt better when you putt as if only your shoulder is swaying.

⑥ You putt better in a slightly open stance.

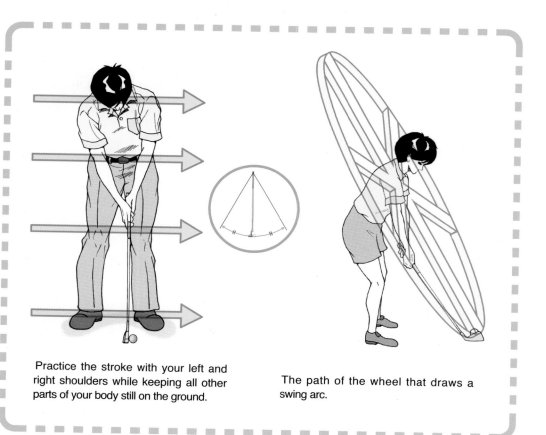

Practice the stroke with your left and right shoulders while keeping all other parts of your body still on the ground.

The path of the wheel that draws a swing arc.

13. The Inside-In Swing Path

Every amateur first learns the inside-out swing. The reason is because the swing path is short. However, when you make a full swing, the club naturally follows an inside-in path.

You should hit, straighten, and turn. Problems arise when you hit and turn without straightening. The cause of this error is that the club does not enter the 'in' path, but the 'out' path.

Therefore, it is very important to move in. For the club to move in, your right knee should not move forward. It should move to the left so that the down swing can move in. When this happens, the support of the left side of your body can shift to the side - support is maintained.

After maintaining support, you should hit, straighten, and turn. In conclusion, if you can form a sound inside-in path, your weight has shifted appropriately.

During this turning process, the problem is how we should move our lower body so that both axes can be supported appropriately. Amateur golfers should try to put the club on the inside path.

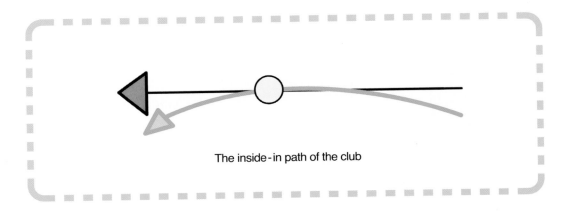

The inside-in path of the club

14. Importance of Maintaining Balance with the Lower Body

Your lower body is the barometer of the accuracy of your golf. As I have emphasized repeatedly, the two axes of the lower body should not move separately, but in correlation with each other.

Your left hip should not be pushed forward during the back swing. Your weight should be shifted internally without any appearance of movement in your lower body. Likewise, during the down swing, your right hip should not move forward before impact, but turn right after the weight shifts to the side.

During the down swing, your weight should also be shifted to the left internally without any external appearance of movement.

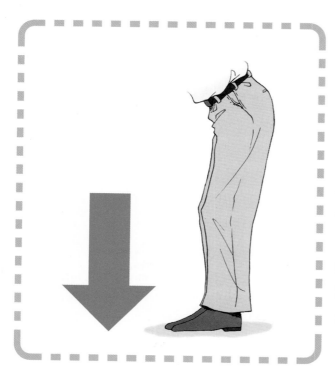

Amateurs can hit a fine, straight ball when they execute the back swing and down swing without any appearance of movement of their lower body.

You need to perceive the importance of your lower body once again, and support it with the two axes as hard as you can.

However, you should also understand that if you try too hard to hit strongly, your support might be compromised.

15. Rhythm and Tempo

Rhythm is a highly important element of golf. Beginners should be particularly aware of rhythm. From an early stage of learning golf, you will try to find your own rhythm.

Put expressively, rhythm is the smooth and unbroken flow of left and right swings from the axis, like a stream of water. The best way to develop sound rhythm is through practice.

Rhythm in golf is largely formed by your shoulder muscles. When you swing the club to the left and right from the axis, and then raise it up, it forms a natural one-piece swing, without any hesitation in the middle. This can be said to be good rhythm. All swings of putters, short approaches, half swings, and full swings should follow a sound rhythm.

For the rhythm of the putter, the key point is a swing of constant tempo. There should be no break in the middle. Any change of speed will break the rhythm.

For a putter or a short approach, the speed of the swing, as well as a constant and rhythmical tempo are the most important things. However short a swing is, you should rest a moment at the end of the back swing, before beginning towards impact.

Different people have different tempos. I have always maintained my own swing's rhythm and tempo. Children's swings should have the tempo of children. There is rhythm and tempo for women, a tempo for male seniors, and a tempo for strong, young men. Each tempo is different.

Women and children may have naturally good rhythms due to the flexibility of their bodies. The same goes for slender men. It is difficult for men with thick bones to develop a smooth rhythm. Therefore, they should cultivate the flexibility of their bodies. Bending your arms a little, and moving your body slightly to the left and right may help your rhythm.

In conclusion, the rhythm of your swing should be a constant flow to the left and right from the axis. It is most important to form a habit out of your own rhythm and tempo. As if playing with the club, practice swinging the club from left to right on the ground, at waist height, and at the shoulder level ten times each a day. This will help you acquire flexibility of body, to feel the rhythm, and develop a constant tempo.

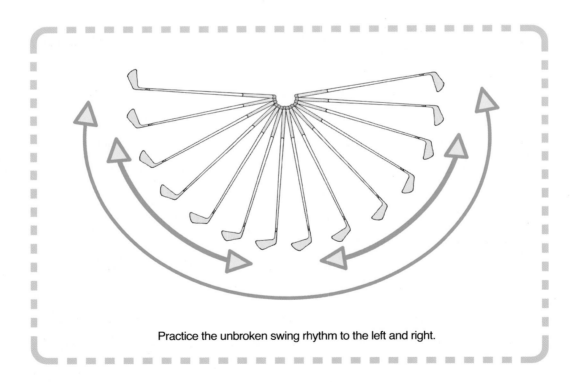

Practice the unbroken swing rhythm to the left and right.

Part 4

USAGE OF CLUBS

1. Driver

Amateur golfers have learned, or will learn soon enough, the importance of a driver shot. For a driver shot, you should pay attention to adjusting the strength of the shot according to your body type.

For strong male professionals, X or S are generally used; for strong male amateurs only S is appropriate; and for general male amateurs, R, R1, or R2 should be considered. Most weak males use an R or regular shaft. Females typically use A or L, the weakest shafts. Stronger females may use an R shaft.

In conclusion, you must choose the shaft strength of a driver that is appropriate for your strength and speed of swing. The lengths of the club, sizes, and materials of the head, and the makers of clubs are very diverse. New models are released on the market, and it can be very difficult to choose one at first. You will need assistance from someone who has some experience.

You may try some clubs and choose the one that feels good to you. Callaway, Honma, Taylormade, and S-yard are widely-known and very popular.

Nowadays, however, you can find many good domestic brands. This makes it easier for you to choose clubs that suit your taste. Furthermore, the driver should be appropriate for your swing speed. If you don't have a very accurate swing path, you should think carefully before choosing the S shaft or a driver with a lower head angle degree such as 9° or 10°. It is not desirable, for example, for a long hitter to use a club with a low-loft head to hit even longer.

The main objective of long hitters should be accuracy of shot, even at the expense of some distance. If your swing speed is slow, the S shaft is inappropriate. If one or two driver shots fall in O.B or hazards, because your angle is lower and the accuracy is poor, it will signal the end of the game for you. The difference between 9° and 10.5° can is akin to that between a spoon and driver.

This brings us to an interesting point : the clubs of 9° and 10.5° have a difference in trajectory. Doesn't this result in a loss of distance?

It is true that the 9° club rolls longer and has a lower trajectory. However, every fair golf player knows that a gain of 10 yards is not greatly important in golf. Accuracy is key in golf. You may use higher or lower angle heads depending on the state of the fairway. The head with a lower angle that produces a lower trajectory and along ground run may be used when the fairway is hard or on a windy day. The head with a higher angle that produces a higher trajectory and longer distances may be more appropriate when the fairway is moist, altitude is high, or when accuracy is paramount.

Almost all amateurs, beginners, mid-level players, or even single handicapped golfers suffer hardship at the hands of the slice of a driver shot. One of the reasons that a slice occurs so often is the high loft of the club. A slice can also occur because the driver is longer than irons and # 3, 4, and 5 woods. So your body turns well before the impact. It can be difficult to bring the long club in so the club goes inside out. Sometimes you may not be able to bring the club close enough to the ground during the initial take back, your whole shoulder does not move in, and you end up making a shot with your arms only. We have already learned about these issues during the swing lessons. Here, however, I will outline some special points regarding the driver.

We all know that a driver shot must be an "upper blow." The blow must be made at the beginning point of upward movement—that is, when the club begins to climb after its lowest point in the swing. (Remind yourself that you should have a sense of hitting the ball while holding it).

You must have heard time and time again: "Swing as if sweeping the floor with a broomstick."

Do not try too hard to hit the ball, but follow through as if pushing the club forward. A hook is also a difficult problem. It happens almost always while your body is standing up.

A further problem with driver shots is the premature winding of your wrist. A larger problem for most people however, is not supporting the left side of their body and 'falling down.' In fact, in order to make a good driver shot, you should be able to play freely with a club that is appropriate for you and your body type.

The components of a perfect driver shot are: good address, adequate stance, natural back swing start, rhythmical and effortless one-piece back swing, spontaneous and smooth down swing, powerful impact of the club moving inside, and a natural finish and follow through.

You can develop the rhythm and sense of a driver by continuously hitting one or two boxes of balls at the driving range. Practice short swings and effortless half swings with a driver.

★ **Precautions for a driver:**

① Always hit the ball with an upper blow not down blow.

② Do not stop after hitting the ball-follow the ball with the club.

③ Do not hit in a hurry-hit calmly.

④ Set a target, and swing towards it.

Driver shot

2. Woods

Asians have different physiques and power levels than Westerners. The Westerners I know are not very tall, but their physique is bigger and very strong.

Therefore, most Asians need to play the woods very well to be a good golfer. Particularly for those with a short and small body or for women, the woods play a large part of their golf. For most female amateurs, for example, the second shot does not fly farther than an iron shot.

Older or weaker men should deal with woods well to get a good score. Depending on the occasion, you many have to use the driver for the second shot. Many beginners avoid using woods out of fear. However, you should be bold—don't be afraid of making errors. Repeated trial and error is the secret to becoming a good player. There are many available selections of wooden clubs. The criteria are similar to those when selecting a driver.

Most golfers use # 3, 4, and 5, and seldom use # 7 and 9 woods. But sometimes # 7 and 9 are necessary, especially for women. Woods are easier to play than irons. The problem is with amateurs thinking that they are more difficult than irons.

You should think that you are swinging woods from side to side. However, even with a wood, you may make a divot after you hit the ball. Hitting at an acute angle could give the ball enough spin to stop on the green. At any rate, the theory of swinging woods is the same as other clubs, and only the position of the ball is different. The most important points for a wood shot are, "Try to hit the ball first," and, "Do not raise the club from the ground too early—form a long follow through along the ground."

You should note that woods are much more convenient than irons, especially for all trouble shots, such as in the rough, and passing through trees. Even in a bunker, if the hill is low, a long second shot may be played with a wood. There are many amateurs who use a wood on a par-3 hole.

Therefore, you need ample practice with woods. For wood practice, the punch shot, sweeping shots, and chopping shots (with the ball moved to the center) are recommended. Soon enough, you will understand the importance of woods on the golf course.

Wood shot

3. Irons

For irons, we will just examine most important points. # 1, 2, 3, and 4 are long irons, # 5, 6, and 7 are middle irons, #8 and 9 are short irons, and then you have pitching wedges and sand wedges. Irons are not used for distance, but for accuracy. Their swing methods are identical to those of other swings, with minor variations. You should be careful of the saying that you should 'chop' irons. If you chop an iron, it may ruin your swing by changing the movement of your body.

The Iron hits the ball right before the lowest point during the down swing. The driver hits the ball at the point where it begins to climb from its lowest point. The wood hits the ball at the lowest point of its swing.

With long irons, however, you should hit the ball at the same position as you do with a wooden club, as if sweeping. With middle irons, you should place the ball at the center of your stance. With short irons, place the ball at the center or one ball's length to the right.

As for club shafts, strong and young players may use steel shafts, or S strength graphite or boron shafts. Most amateurs typically use regular strength shafts.

Women can use the lady shaft set for women's strength. Since there are so many club makers, you may need advice from someone who plays golf.

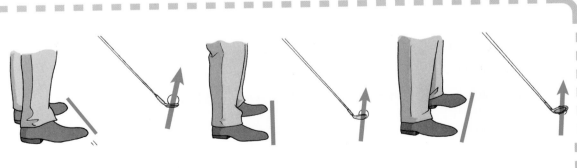

Open Stance of Short Iron   Square Stance of Middle Iron   Draw Stance of Long Iron

1) Shot by Iron Type

(1) Long irons are long and their heads have steepen angles. Therefore, it is not easy to make impact squarely. You need to play a side blow to make correct impact. With long clubs, slice shots are common because the impact tends to come behind the body in the down swing. You need to make a sweeping blow, rather than a down blow so that the head can hit the ball at a right angle at the point of impact. Furthermore, the swing should be effortless and followed through fully.

(2) Middle irons are better for achieving accuracy, distance and direction than any other iron. These are also the most practiced clubs, so fewer errors tend to be made. For both long and middle irons, your shoulders should turn sufficiently, and the back swing should not travel too far back. During the down swing, the lead of your lower body is important. When you hit the ball during the down blow, you should retain the sense of resting for a brief moment at impact. The impact should be bold.

(3) With short irons, the key points are a sufficient turn of the shoulder, the lead of the lower body during the down swing, and a follow through wherein the club follows the ball after impact. The follow through must be solid. You should be more careful not to bring your head up when using shorter clubs, and your stance must be narrow for a smooth shift of weight.

(4) Pitching should be done with the same swing as the short irons. You should guard against a shot with your arms only–this will result in a hooked shot. With shorter clubs, if the finish is too big, the target direction of the swing will be incorrect.

(5) Sand shots require a solid follow through, like a full swing. The impact point is

actually about 5cm or less behind the ball, and you should swing the club as if scooping up sand with a shovel.

(6) From long irons to chipping, remember that the swing of all irons should be made with a sufficient turn of the shoulders. The down swing must be made using the club as if part of the same body as your shoulder. During follow through, your right shoulder must follow in.

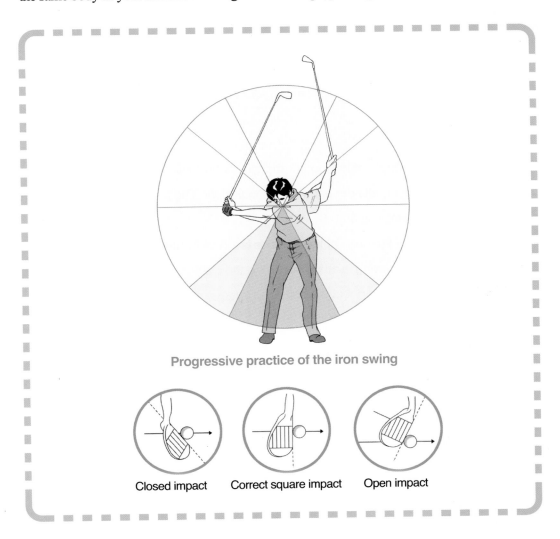

Progressive practice of the iron swing

Closed impact   Correct square impact   Open impact

4. Putter

A par golf game consists of 36 shots and 36 putts. In other words, putting represents half of the golf score. (This calculation assumes two putts per hole, over 18 holes.) Therefore, your choice of putter is vital to your game.

For amateurs, a heavier putter is better than a lighter one. In general, 320 to 340 grams of head weight is preferable. Many people use the putters of famous brands. The shapes include the L-type, T-type, Goose Neck type, and the Half-moon type. Try some and choose the shape that feels right for you, along with the help of your golfing friend. The length of the putter should be appropriate for your height. Choose a putter that seems to be preferred by many people.

① The best address angle of putting, for the direction of the stroke, is about 70° from the ground. However, this depends on the individual. The putter's lie angle is about 70°, and the face angle is 3° to 6°.

② The best position of the head at the address is 1.5 to 2 putter heads from your foot.

③ The size of the back swing is proportionate to the distance from the target. The best position of the ball is straight down from your left eye at the address.

④ Back spin of the putt shortens the distance, and top spin makes the ball roll better.

⑤ When there is no loft angle for putting, the ball bounds and direction and distance are compromised. Therefore, you should stroke without changing the loft angle.

⑥ Rhythm, tempo, impact, shoulder-only swings, and no movement of the wrist are all vital elements of sound putting.

⑦ Above all, clear your mind, and concentrate fully on the putt to achieve success.

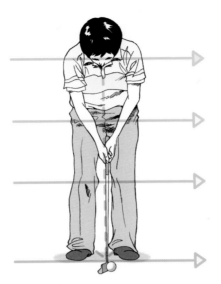

Correct putting address

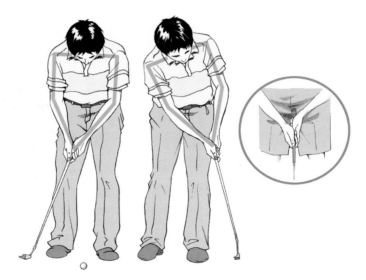

The arms naturally form a pentagon, and the back swing and follow through are symmetrical. The swing should always be made from the shoulder.

Sound putting : the back swing and the follow through have the same distance

Incorrect putting : a short back swing and a long follow through

Incorrect putting : a long back swing and a short follow through

The latest popular reverse grip stroke, where the left wrist does not bend

1. Pitching Approach

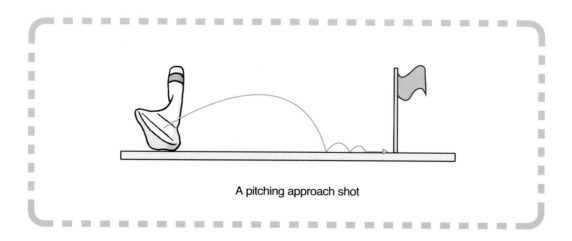

A pitching approach shot

Pitching is to fly the ball to approach the pin. At the approach, pitching requires accuracy before anything else. Most amateurs have difficulties pitching due to the following reasons :

Firstly, a hooked shot occurs in many cases.
Secondly, the shot falls short and does not approach the pin.
Thirdly, the back swing is big, while the follow through is small.

1) First Case

Because the club is short, the swing becomes too fast and the follow through becomes one like in a regular swing. This causes a hook. In order to hit a straight ball, you should stretch the club head to the pin at finish, even if the finish is incomplete.

2) Second Case

You should always play towards the flag in the hole-cup to make the distance. You need to make your stroke as if sending the ball over the flag.

3) Third Case

If you have not practiced adjusting the size of your back swing, it often automatically becomes too big. Since the pin is only a short distance away, if you try to reduce power when making your shot, you may hit the ground or commit topping. This is because you are playing with your arms, not your shoulders. You should play with the turn of your shoulders.

Always keep these above three points in mind. And let me add a few more key points : hold the grip firmly ; do not bend your wrist at impact ; hold your club down during follow through. For pitching, a pitching wedge or # 9 iron is usually used. You can also use a sand wedge. However, most amateurs fear the sand wedge.

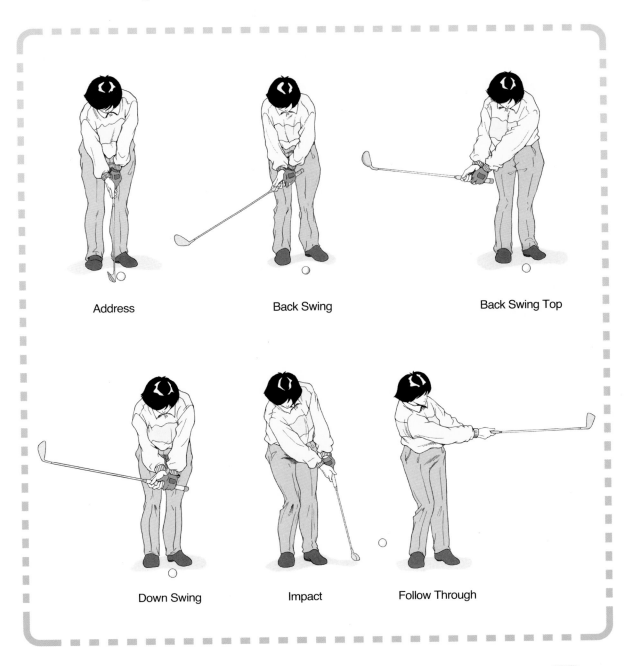

Address

Back Swing

Back Swing Top

Down Swing

Impact

Follow Through

2. Pitch and Run

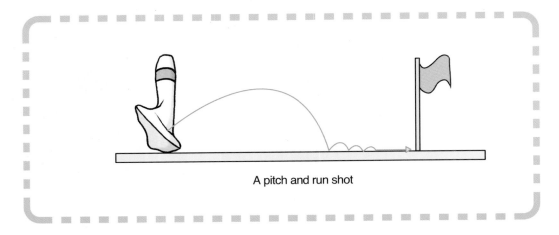

A pitch and run shot

This shot is a special weapon for amateurs. A pitch and run shot is made with a pitching wedge or a sand wedge. The ball drops and rolls to the pin.

This shot varies according to the season, and the state and slant of the green. You can also create various angles with the club. A feel is more important than technique here.

It takes a lot of practice to determine the correct angle for impact and the right size of shot. Much experience and a smart mind are required to be able to grasp the differences by season and slant of green. The accuracy of your approach depends on where the ball falls and begins its run. You should adjust for the distance with the degree of follow through.

Grip the club firmly and lower than usual, make bold impact, and always throw the club toward the hole-cup. Only your shoulder should move during the swing while your lower body remains perfectly still. Your wrist should not bend.

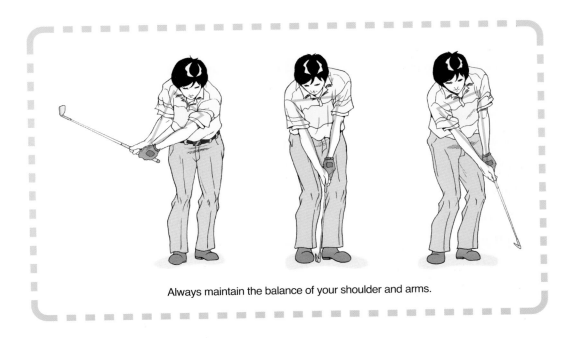

Always maintain the balance of your shoulder and arms.

3. Running Approach

Amateurs usually use an approach around the green, but I was called ʻthe master of the running approachʼ by my friends. You may use one of many clubs depending on the

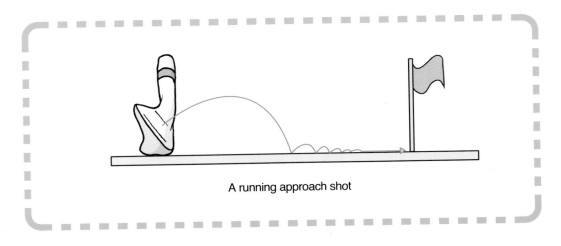

A running approach shot

situation. Irons # 8, 7, 6, and 5 are all suitable.

How far the ball runs is determined by the power of impact, and the size of the follow through. A sense of the shot is also of paramount importance as the conditions of the green always change.

On a level field or down hill, # 8 or 9 should be used. If the distance is small on a slightly raised green, you may use # 7. On a two-step green where there is a rise in the middle, or on a long, narrow raised green, or on a green with long lawn where the ball does not run well, # 6 is appropriate. If the pin is at the back of the green, and the green is steeply uphill, you may use # 5 or even # 4 to run the ball uphill to the pin.

All these tactics for placing the ball to the right position cannot be formularized. They are best learned through experience. In other words, you should try every club in every situation. In addition, you should hold the club firmly, impact should be bold, and your lower body should be fixed like a pole rooted in the ground. Only your upper body should move during the shot ; then the motion of your lower body will be just right.

A running shot is particularly effective in late autumn or winter.

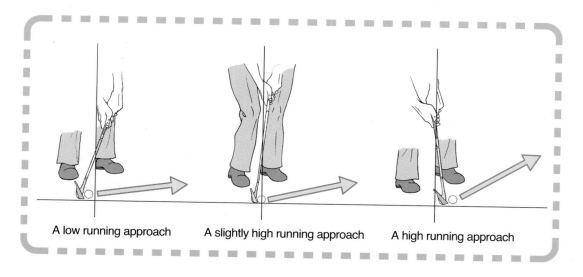

A low running approach   A slightly high running approach   A high running approach

Part 6

BUNKERS AROUND THE GREEN

A bunker shot is one of the worst fears for most amateurs and beginners. There are good reasons for this.

First of all, few amateurs have mastered their swing arc. If the swing arc is solid and the follow through is made naturally until the finish, bunker shots should offer very few problems. Another reason for the fear of bunkers is lack of confidence. Amateurs tend to cut short the follow through, because they fear that the ball will fly too far if they play a normal shot. In short, amateurs do not make a full follow through, for fear of a long shot.

The third problem is that some players do not hit the right position. They often hit the back of the ball by swaying their bodies, or hit the ball head-on by moving their head up.

Since your feet are in the sand and can be easily swayed, you should rub your feet deeply into the sand for firm support. Your swing should move outside in, with impact at about 5cm behind the ball. Make a bold shot, with the feeling that your follow through is longer than the back swing. If you keep these things in mind, bunker shots will become very easy for you. What is difficult is adjusting for different distances.

You can adjust for distance in two ways : by the quantity of sand dipped out, or by running according to the angle of the club. In most cases, you can determine distance by the size of your back swing and the quantity of sand. This method is safe for you. Remember: a follow through to the finish is most important for amateurs.

There are other difficult bunker shots: when the ball is in a deep bunker near the green, or in a bunker 20 to 30 yards from the green.

The shot from a deep bunker requires some technique. The down swing should be made at an acute angle, and the follow through should be made over a steep slope so that the ball can fly high. The explosive power of a V-shot is necessary here.

The most difficult shot is from a bunker farther than 20 to 30 yards from the green.

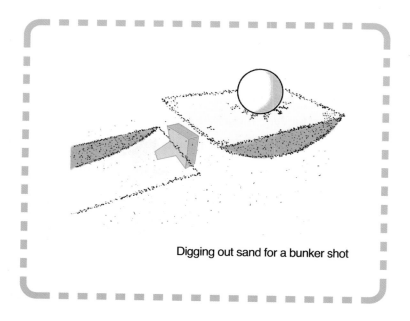

Digging out sand for a bunker shot

If the bunker is rather far, you can use a # 9, with a sharper blade, or even a # 7. The head angle should be sufficiently acute in order for you to make a running shot without digging out too much sand. Therefore, you don't always have to use a sand club for a bunker shot. You need to take all these points into account every time and spend time to think about these points. Don't be afraid to think for yourself.

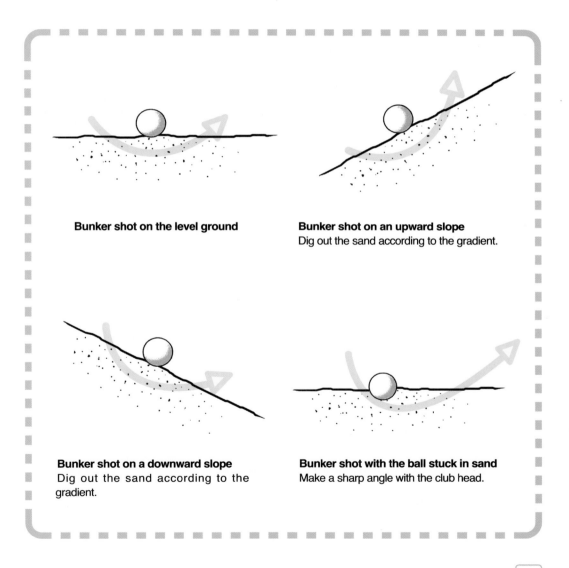

Bunker shot on the level ground

Bunker shot on an upward slope
Dig out the sand according to the gradient.

Bunker shot on a downward slope
Dig out the sand according to the gradient.

Bunker shot with the ball stuck in sand
Make a sharp angle with the club head.

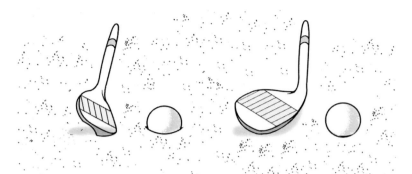

When the ball is stuck in sand
Make a sharp angle with the club head.

When the ball is sitting on the sand
Make a wide angle with the club head.

★ ☆ ★ Terms of Golf Lessons

① During the first 6 months, you should concentrate on learning the circular path of the swing and cultivate flexibility in each part of your body.

② During the second 6 months, you should gradually develop the overall sense of golf swings, such as a full swing, short swings, and putting.

During the second year, you will learn the techniques of golf. During this period, you will have various experiences, and make many errors, including poor swings.

④ During the third year, after you have enjoyed many good and bad experiences, you need to get two thorough lessons per year to master your own swing, having developed your own gut feeling of what is right and wrong.

⑤ After 3 years, keep practicing your swing to maintain the proper form, while receiving point lessons.

Part 7.

CROSS BUNKERS

You really need to make a clean hit. In order to achieve this, your lower body should not sway, and you should select a club one or two steps longer, holding it shorter than usual.

You will make a poor shot if your grip is released too early, if your body moves up and down, or if your feet are not firmly supported in the sand.

In order to get the ball out easily, you should choose a club according to the situation. When the lie is good and the rise is low, you may use a wood.

Even if the hill is near, you may use an iron if the ball's lie is good. If you think that the rise is too high and you can't get the ball out, use a wedge or a # 9 iron. If the ball is stuck in the sand, use a sand wedge.

A bunker shot with feet deep in the sand to keep them from moving

Part 8.

PUTTING

1. Grasping the Putting Green

1) If you have gotten the ball onto the green or at the green's edge, the first thing you should do is have a good look at the green and try to grasp the situation. Look for irregularities on the green, and note the slant between your ball and the hole-cup.

2) The running of the ball varies according to the length of grass. Well-managed grass is short, and the ball runs well. The running also depends on the direction of the grass. If the grass runs contrary to the ball's intended direction, the ball will not run well. Furthermore, if there is water near the green, the ball will run faster nearer to the water. You should consider all these conditions when putting.

3) The slant of the green also varies a great deal. Sometimes there are two-level greens to contend with. Some greens have many ups and downs. You need to cope with all these variations. As a rule of thumb, you need to play to the higher ground on a side slant, cautiously downhill, and boldly uphill.

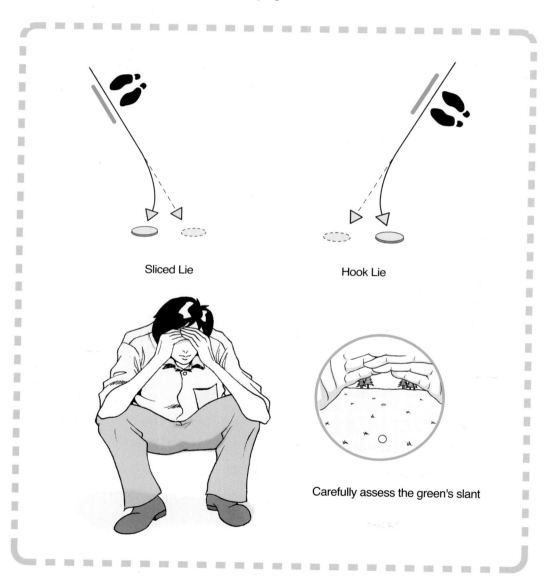

Sliced Lie

Hook Lie

Carefully assess the green's slant

2. The Feel of Good Putting

Everything in golf requires a sense of the right touch and feel. Putting in particular requires a raw instinct. In the beginning, amateur golfers need to practice to get the right feel.

The most important things in putting are the prevention of tenseness in hands at impact, a natural back swing, and no bending of the wrists during the follow through. If you master these techniques, you should putt well.

Although direction is more to do with geometry than gut feeling, determining the actual distance is more an ability of instinct and experience than calculation. There are two kinds of golfers : some get the sense of distance from the strength of impact and others from the feeling of follow through. Most people belong to the latter group.

For long putting, you can obtain a better sense of distance if you stand taller than you would for a short putt. So keep your back straighter than usual. Relax your mind and play prudently.

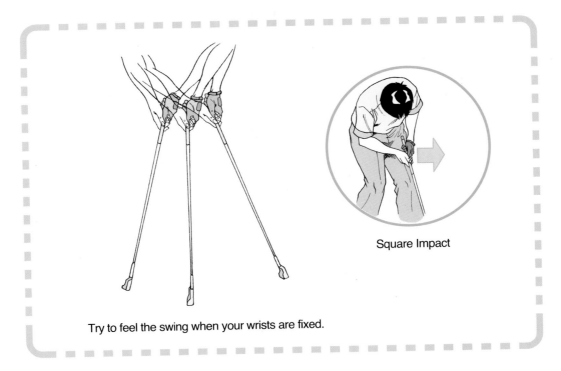

Square Impact

Try to feel the swing when your wrists are fixed.

3. Variables in Putting

1) The run of the ball and the state of the green changes from season to season. The ball runs well in spring and autumn. Many greens are not level during winter. Greens are usually better kept in late spring, summer, and early autumn.
However, the lawn on the green cannot be mown during the change of season from autumn to winter. Therefore, the ball may not run well due to longer grass. Furthermore, sometimes sand is spread on the green to protect the grass, and in the morning, you may find it difficult to putt because the sand is wet from morning dew.

2) Each golf course has different green conditions. Some have the green mowed short, and manage it well. Others don't mow the green often because they are afraid the grass may die.

3) Around summer when the weather is good, the ball may not run well in the morning because of morning dew. It will run well during the day, but by the evening it may not run as well because the grass has grown. In strong winds, or when it is raining, the ball will not run well when there is rain or a headwind. The ball will run too well with a tailwind.

4) One of the difficulties of putting is the ratio of the speed of the ball against the slant of the green. If the ball speed is too high, the bend will be too small. If ball speed is too low, the bend will be too great. Furthermore, if there is a downhill slope after an uphill slope, strength control is extremely difficult. There are also steep downward sloping hills, for which just a little touch will result in the ball traveling very far. On the other hand, you need to play straight ahead on such a slope where the left is

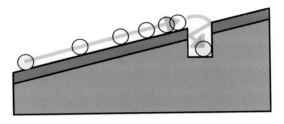

For putting uphill, play boldly so that the ball will hit the rear part of the hole and bounce back in.

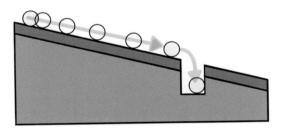

For putting downhill, play cautiously so that the ball will naturally fall into the hole.

slightly high, and then the right is also high. You need to practice on your own to overcome all these difficulties.

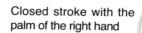
Closed stroke with the
palm of the right hand

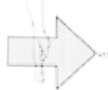

Square stroke with
the palm of the right
hand

Open stroke with the
palm of the right hand

★☆★ **The conditions for distance and direction**

① Swing path (in, square, in)

② Position of the club face (square position)

③ Swing spot impact

④ Swing speed

⑤ Support of the lower body

Part 9.

TROUBLE SHOTS

1. Uphill Lies

Typically in this situation, the ground is slanted from the left foot to the right foot. Therefore, you should bend your left foot a great deal. You don't need to bend your right foot to form a sound stance. When you stand like this, your shoulders should be parallel to the slanted ground, so that you can make the swing arc appropriately. The ball will fly in a high trajectory like the slanted ground, and you should follow through with your club in accordance with the path of the ball and the slant.

The ball should split the distance between your feet, and you should hold a one-or two-step longer grip, depending on the situation. If the ball flies high, you can reduce the distance by shortening the grip. What amateurs need to know in this situation is that each player should have his/her own sense of the right thing to do. Some experimentation is essential.

In my case, it is easier to hit the ball straight if I raise my body upon impact and send the club in the direction of the ball. If you try to play in accordance with the slant while standing still, it is difficult to hit the ball in the right direction.

"Since the ball tends to hook when playing uphill, play a little to the right." This advice does not apply well to amateurs. Instead of a full finish, if you push the club further to the target direction, the ball will fly straight. In short, for amateurs, making a shot with techniques for coping with the natural conditions is more important than formulas.

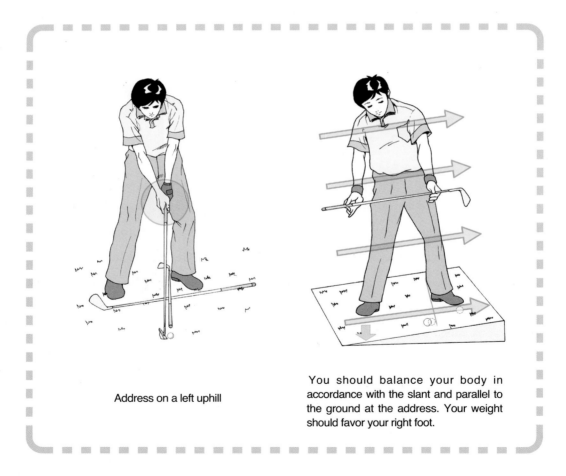

Address on a left uphill

You should balance your body in accordance with the slant and parallel to the ground at the address. Your weight should favor your right foot.

2. Downhill Lies

If you understand the concept of the left upward slope, it will be easier for you to understand the concept of the left downward slope—they are exact opposites. As the slope is slanted to the left, you should incline your shoulders with the ground. Your stance should be slightly wider. Moreover, you should straighten your left foot, and bend your right foot to make a swing path that corresponds to the slant. Keep the ball in the center, and choose a club that is one-or two-steps shorter. Form a downward finish in accordance with the slant. Since the trajectory is low, even if you use a one-or two-step shorter club, you will gain a one-or two-club distance advantage.

Similarly, the shot can be played differently depending on the player. As for myself, I raise the club almost directly in accordance with the slant, and finish with a low follow through. If I swing slightly downward at impact, rather than directly from above, I achieve a lower error rate. The most common error is hitting the ground behind the ball. As for direction, amateurs can hit a better straight ball if they follow through, by following the ball with the club, rather than targeting to the left of the target to cope with the slice.

To be sure, if the slant is steep, you need to consider the possibility of slice. Bear in mind that you should make adjustments according to the natural conditions. I will explain more in detail later about the differences between clubs. In any case, you will surely make a sound shot, if the slant of your club is consistent with that of the ground.

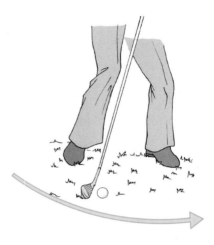

Balance your body in conformity with the slant of the ground.

Place more weight on the left foot and make a low follow through.

★☆★ **Major Tournament**

U.S. Masters
The U.S. Masters was founded in 1934 by Bob Jones, an amateur American golfer. The competition is held in the second week of April every year at Augusta National Golf Club in USA.

U.S. Open
This competition is held in June every year.

British Open
This competition is held in July in Britain every year.

US PGA Championships
This competition is held in August every year. Only pro golfers from all over the world may participate.
There are four players to have won all four major competitions : Jack Nicklaus, Gary Player, Ben Hogan, and Gene Sarasen.

3. Ball Above Stance

In short, this is a trouble shot. The most important thing for a trouble shot is to maintain a fixed and motionless lower body. For a front-upward-slope shot, straighten your body and knees, and use a one- or two-steps longer club. Hold the club shorter, and adjust the hitting distance at the address. Firmly support yourself with your lower body, form a short back swing, and watch and hit the ball accurately. For the follow through, the best thing you can do as an amateur is to follow the ball with your club, and swing as for a half-swing.

In terms of direction, look straight ahead or a little to the right. You need to adopt a sense of following the ball at impact. Shift your weight in the ball's direction.

For the front-upward-slope shot, hold the club short and straighten the knees.

4. Ball Below Stance

This is the opposite shot to the front upward slope.

You should straighten your knees, shift your weight to your heels, and hold the club longer than you would on level ground. Do not straighten your legs or move your feet. Form the back swing and the follow through as half swings, not full swings.

Since the ball may often be sliced, you may target slightly to the left of the target. On the follow through, follow the ball with the club.

One thing to ensure is that you hit the ball without any motion of your lower body. Ensure up and down movement is kept to a minimum.

Address for the front - downward - slope shot.
Shift your weight to your heels.

5. Ball Above Stance Uphill

This shot refers to when you are standing on an uphill and the ball is situated on the right uphill.

In contrast to foreign golf courses, where there are many level fields, golf courses in Korea were often built on mountains, or from small mountains leveled off. Subsequently, there are often many holes where the right side is higher. This shot must be made similarly to the front upward slope. In general, however, you will be targeting the green on your left. Unfortunately, in this case, the hole is high and curved to the right. Thankfully, this should become a rare shot you will have to make.

For this kind of slope, you don't need a standard pose or regular swing. Your back swing should be especially smooth. You should not use your lower body. Do not take too big of a swing, and follow the ball with your eyes all the way. Swing your club with the sense that you are throwing your body.

The most frequent miss in this situation is to hit the ground behind the ball. (Amateurs often insist that it was just a practice shot!)

Another problem is that even though it should be easy to send the ball to the fairway since you are hitting downward from a hill, the ball may continue flying up the mountain. This happens if your body moves too early and your club is let to drop. Furthermore, a bad hook swing may occur if you are too tense, or if your body is not well supported. You need to firmly support your body and move graciously.

Maintain these principles for the front upward shot: watch the ball closely, and follow the ball until finish while targeting the flag.

6. Ball Below Stance Uphill

These troubles shots require us to make variations to the basic principles, because the degrees of slope are always different.

Unlike professional golfers, who have mastered the principles, amateurs don't have much experience handling trouble shots, and don't have the opportunity to practice them a great deal. Therefore, the capability to cope with variations in their own way is required of amateur golfers.

Especially in Korea, where there are many uphill holes, you will meet many difficult situations on the golf course. These include making shots when there is a left wall on an uphill slope. In this particular case, the slope is uphill to the left, downhill to the front, and the hole is to your right. In this situation, the possibility of a hook or slice is considerable. If the green is on the left, you should be careful of a hooked shot. If the green is on the right, the possibility of a sliced shot is almost 100%: in this case, therefore, you should make your shot by targeting to the left of the green, allowing for the near-certainty of a sliced shot.

In this case also, your club should be stretched to the flag's direction during follow through. Shift your weight just enough so that you can throw the club, and form a small back swing. Never raise your upper body.

7. Ball Above Stance Downhill

There is a golf course on the outskirts of Seoul that I used to frequent where you need to handle numerous trouble shots, such as front high lies or front downward slopes.

One particular hole is on a downward slope, where the ball is near the right wall, and you need to target the green on your left. As described above, you should hold the club a little shorter, try not to make the swing too big, and adjust the path of swing to the slope. You should also pay firm attention to the direction of your shot.

If the green is on the right, you can target directly ahead, forming a rather short follow through to the flag's direction. However, if the green is on the left, you should target slightly to the right, forming a smooth, relaxed swing.

The position of the ball should be slightly to the right of the center line between your feet. Follow the ball all the way, and try not to move your body. Otherwise, you will slice or hook the ball.

8. Ball Below Stance Downhill

This situation occurs when the ball is near the left wall on a downward hole, or near an undulation (ups and downs on the course) on a downward fairway. The ball is therefore lower than, and in front of, your feet.

Since the front is low, you need to bend your knees considerably to form a low pose. Target to the left of the green in anticipation of a sliced shot.

You always need to picture the swing in accordance with the slope. Topping is common because amateurs tend to move their back swing up or down too much. If you do not stretch the club straight, the slice will be larger or a hook will result.

As always for trouble shots, ensure you do not make too big of a swing, or move your body too much. Play the shot with a sense rather than a principle, watch the ball closely, and follow through in the flag's direction.

9. Rough

The area between the tee and the green is called the fairway. The area on both sides of the fairway where the grass is neglected is called the rough.

In Korea, there are many trees by the rough. Many different conditions can be found under the trees, such as long grass or bare ground. As golfers, we need to be able to cope with these diverse conditions.

The condition of the rough may also change with the seasons. In summer, the grass is longer, and it is difficult to hit the ball in the rough. In winter, the grass is laid flat down, and it is relatively easy to hit the ball. It is important to choose the right club according to the situation. Depending on the situation, a wood may be easier to swing than an iron in some rough.

Sometimes, making a shot in the rough means you have to cut the grass with the club before hitting the ball. Hitting the ball in long grass will inevitably result in an error. Since it is easier to cut the grass if the blades are standing rather than lying down, it is better to choose a one-step shorter club. Your wrist must stand firm, and your club should easily slip forward above the ground, rather than close to the ground.

You should form a shot that cuts the grass and then carries the ball out. Therefore, if the grass is tough and not too long, a wood is much easier to swing. If the ground under a tree is bare, you will make fewer errors if you make a short swing with a wood, rather than an iron. In particular, when you must pass the ball past a tree under the branches, a wood is more convenient.

Bear in mind all these things when you make a shot from the rough. The most important things are the strength of your wrists and ensuring that your body does not move forward. A Strong impact is also required.

10. Hazards

Yellow or red poles are placed in water or damp areas where the ball can't be played. Players are given one penalty shot when their ball falls in these areas. If the ball falls inside the red pole regardless of the spot, the player must drop the ball around the tee off position, or at the entrance to the hazard. The red poles are put in lateral water hazards, (rivers or lakes running alongside the fairway), or in damp areas in the mountains.

When your ball falls in these hazards, you should drop the ball within two club lengths from the side of the hazard, and you are given one penalty stroke. If you can make a shot in the hazard, you may do so, but the club must not touch the ground.

If your ball falls in a pond in the middle of the fairway and the area has a yellow pole, you should play the shot from the nearside of the pond, irrespective of where the ball landed. Alternatively, you can replay the shot from the original position. In this case, it is considered the third shot.

Bunkers are also hazards. The same rules apply to them. Your club should not touch the ground. You may play from the bunker if possible.

You should obviously do your best not to send the ball into hazards.

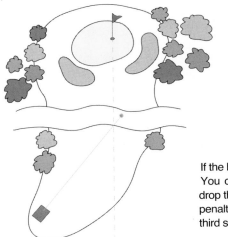

Water Hazard

If the ball falls in a water hazard :
You can play from the same place again, or drop the ball near the water. In either case, one penalty shot is given to you. This is now your third shot.

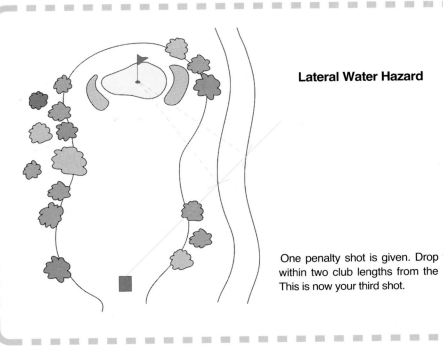

Lateral Water Hazard

One penalty shot is given. Drop the ball within two club lengths from the hazard. This is now your third shot.

If there is water in the bunker, you can drop the ball within one club length from the water without penalty. However, the ball must be dropped inside the bunker no nearer to the flag.

★☆★ **Greens higher or lower than the tee ground :**

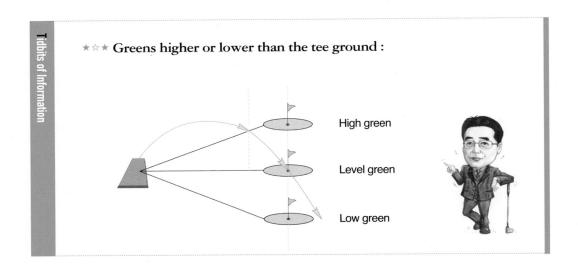

High green

Level green

Low green

11. Lob Shot Over a Tree

When I discuss making shots over a tree, under the blue sky and the silky clouds as white as snow, I feel as if I am talking about the world as seen through the eyes of a child.

In order for the ball to fly, you should not move your body forward before impact. Doing so causes a sharp angle of the club, resulting in a low trajectory. Keep your body steady to maintain the angle of the club at impact, so as to create a high trajectory of flight. The ball will then fly in the same angle as that of the club face, be it a # 9, a pitching wedge, or a sand wedge.

If the trees are considerably tall, and it seems very difficult to pass the ball over them, you may enlarge the angle of the club by holding it down as an expedient. For example, if you suspect that even though a # 9 iron is right for the distance, it would fall short due to the high trees, you can use a # 8 iron by laying it down.

Whenever you need to hit the ball over tall trees, the most important thing is that your upper and lower body should maintain their balance and not move at impact. Likewise, when you have to pass the ball across the trees in the O.B area on a downward slope to the green, it is absolutely essential that your body does not fall forward. Otherwise, you will never pass the ball over the trees.

To conclude, the most important thing is to support your body at the point of impact in order to maintain the trajectory of the club.

12. Punch Shot Under a Tree

A punch shot is one in which you hit the ball under, or through, the branches of a tree.

The most vital issue is to form a low follow through after impact. In contrast to the flying shot, your club should not be laid down. The angle of the club must be steep. Even if your body is pushed slightly forward, this will not unduly influence the shot.

This is not to say that you should intentionally move your body forward. But if you do, it is better than flying the ball-remember, in this case, your main goal is to keep the ball beneath and around the bulk of the tree. You have to use a one-step shorter iron, straighten the club up, and form a low follow through. Depending on the height of the tree, you should form a follow through lower than a half-swing.

Also bear in mind that your arms should not be bent. They should be stretched straight at impact. Sometimes it can be a good idea to use a wood.

13. Bare Ground

You can see a lot of bare ground in old golf courses, where the grass is not well maintained during late autumn, winter, and early spring.

One golf course on the outskirts of Seoul is all but completely bare ground. I can say this because I have frequented it for 12 years.

Even on this kind of golf course, bare ground is not a major problem. However, if the ground is muddy or crumbly, you should be careful about hitting it when you hit the ball. Short approaches can also be more difficult. Sometimes, there is a lot of bare ground in the O.B areas among big trees and the rough before the poles. This happens because the grass cannot grow among large trees.

In all the situations when dealing with bare ground strokes, one thing to be most careful of is pushing the club forward after striking the ball. If you make a "V" shot, the club will most likely hit the ground. For this kind of shot, where your wrists are released early, and the club head moves to the ball before your wrists, the head must follow behind the wrists, as if it is pulled. This creates a situation in which the head will push forward as it hits the ball.

In other words, your club should hit the ball first, and then pass forward. Of course, planning to hit the ball first and then pass the club forward is easier than the execution. Planning is not enough. You should not release your wrists and make a shot as if pulling in further. This would likely cause a missed shot. In this manner, the ball does not fly high. Another way to make fewer misses is to have the ball slightly to the right of center.

★ ☆ ★ The paths of the ball

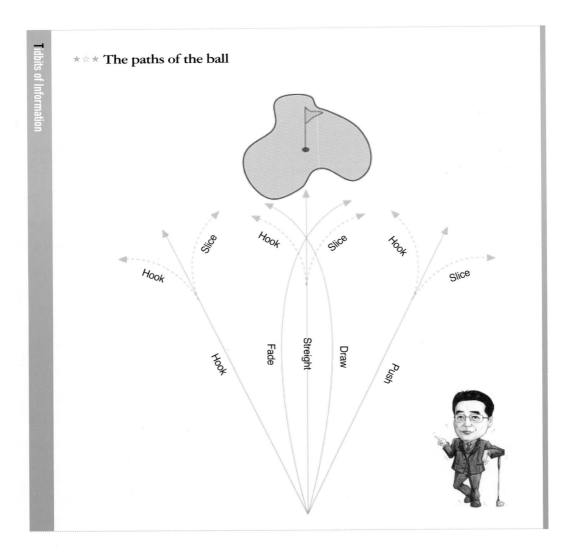

Part 10.

FIGHTING AGAINST NATURE

1. Wind

When I was a beginner, my play was adversely affected by wind. Even to this day, the wind can cause me to miss shots.

The wind can blow from any direction. You can tell the direction of the wind by the fluttering of the flag. Wind greatly affects your shot, and it can help when it blows from behind because it makes the ball fly farther. The speed of wind also influences the flying distance of balls.

A head wind is the enemy of all golfers. If a strong head wind blows when you are about to make a tee shot, you have to think seriously about placing the tee low and shooting a low trajectory shot. Your aim is to play through the wind.

If you think too much at the tee shot, you cannot concentrate. Consequently you will backswing too quickly, and miss the shot. However, an experienced player can relax their mind, and calmly place the tee lower.

For winds blowing from left to right, you should target slightly to the left, depending on the speed of the wind. It often happens that even when you play a shot to the left because of the wind, the ball is not greatly affected by wind.

Amateurs always complain, "Why doesn't the ball ride the wind? I targeted left to accommodate for the wind, but⋯." Most golfers understand the difficulties involved in making an accurate shot after taking wind into consideration.

Amateurs cannot but depend on their sense on how much to the right they should target when the wind is blowing right to left.

If they miscalculate, they can simply say, "The wind was not as strong as I thought⋯." I once got the ball 160 meters onto the green with a driver on a golf course on Jeju Island thanks to the wind. We need to look at the wind positively. If we take it easy and think, "I will just play once more to get onto the green," we will usually make a better shot.

In short, the greatest threat that wind presents any amateur golfer is the unsettling of our concentration.

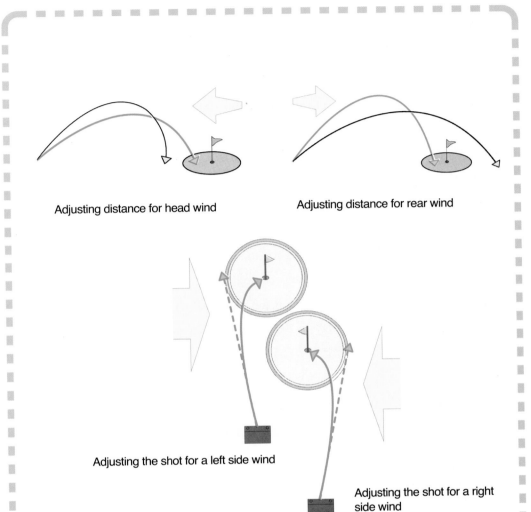

Adjusting distance for head wind

Adjusting distance for rear wind

Adjusting the shot for a left side wind

Adjusting the shot for a right side wind

2. Rain

Rain is also the enemy of concentration. In your days as a beginner, rain makes you hurry, and your shots are often played faster and rougher. As you gain in experience, your mind will be calm, rain or shine.

Depending on the rainfall, choose a one-or two-step longer club. If the ground is wet, wrist support must be stronger.

If it begins raining as you start your round, you should have few problems if you prepared in advance. You do need, however, to take special care on the day after rainfall, especially if it looks like it has completely cleared up.

Sometimes, the ground appears OK but the club can get stuck in it. You cannot play golf if it snows, but you can play in light rain as long as water does not stay on the green.

One helpful tip for playing in the rain is that real cotton gloves are the least slippery. The real enemy of a round of golf played in the rain is lost concentration. Another tip is that it is usually better to hit the ball upwards.

3. Bunkers

It often happens that even with your greatest efforts to evade a bunker, the ball falls into it. When this happens, you need some luck. If the ball is on the front or back hill, you have no choice but to play backwards, and attempt to escape the bunker at the next shot.

If the ball falls at an area in the bunker from which you can swing more comfortably, you need to bury your feet in the sand so that you can stand firmly, and fix your lower body. Moreover, your knees and waist should not be stretched or bent during a shot. Your wrists should not be released early. This results in a downward swing, and a missed shot. If your up-and-down motion is greater than your left-and-right motion, you will not be able to hit the ball. You will more often than not hit the sand behind the ball instead.

You need to be able to hit the exact impact point at the center of the ball. With this kind of shot, you must realize the importance of accuracy of your body movement.

Bunker shots are no different from fairway shots, but they do require more attention. Since the ground is sand, it does not support your strength well, whichever direction you exert it. Therefore, you first step is to settle yourself firmly in the sand to support yourself well.

Remember the concept of hitting the ball first. It is not difficult to escape from a bunker. In a bunker, you need to have the confidence to use a driver, or even a spoon!

The ball is far away from the front hill. You can play with a wood.

The ball is in a cross bunker, and still quite a distance from the front hill. You can play with a middle iron.

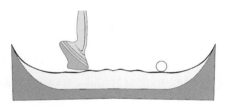

The ball is near the front hill in a cross bunker. You can play with a short iron.

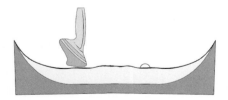

The ball is buried in sand. You should use a sand wedge to escape from the bunker.

4. Change of Seasons

Playing golf is very different from season to season. You can enjoy a new experience and new challenges with each season.

1) Spring

When spring comes, many people wish to test the golfing abilities that they have cultivated throughout the winter. However, when you actually play golf in spring, you may often feel that you cannot score well, and that your shots are not as good as you wished them to be. In fact, more often than not, the spring season is associated with many errors, such as duffs and topping. The reality of golf in spring is far from your general feelings of joy in the warm weather and blooming flowers.

The problem is the condition of the ground. The grass is not fully grown yet, the ground is hard and dry, and the ball falls more often on bare ground than on grass. In these conditions, your club does not swing well, and it is hard to play a straight shot because it is difficult to form right angles between the face of the club and the ball. If your second shot went crooked, place your hopes on the approach. The approach shot is no easy task either. When the green is perfect, it is easy enough to get the ball near the hole-cup, if you just follow through softly as you do at the driving range. In spring, however, the ground around the green is neither bare nor grass, and it is difficult to achieve the desired distance with a clean shot. You can avoid a duff shot if you hit the ball harder than usual—but this makes it more difficult to get the distance right. Moreover, when sand is scattered around the green, the ground is harder. If the short grass is not leveled with a roller, the ball will not run well. All these factors contribute to global golfer disappointment in spring.

However, even under the most severe conditions, our desire for improvement should not cease.

2) Summer

Summer provides the best conditions for playing golf, except for the extreme heat of midsummer. The grass on the fairways and the greens are in good shape, and the body is more supple than in any other season. We score our lowest scores and our sense of play is enhanced by the favorable conditions. We have to make use of the summer as the season to restore our confidence and savor the essence of golf.

Even if it rains often in the summer, a round of golf is possible as long as water does not stay on the green. This is in sharp contrast to the winter months, when golf cannot be played if snow is covering the green.

You do, however, need to be particularly careful of the rough in summer. The rough is always the enemy of a summer round of golf. Since the grass is tall, the club often falls below the ball at the approach. This results in a flying shot, and shorter distance shots. Furthermore, on the day after rain when the ground appears OK, but is damp underneath, your club can get stuck in the ground−resulting in a duff shot. You should be careful of these pitfalls in summer.

3) Autumn

Autumn is the season of abundance and harvest. Golf in the autumn is pleasant, but provides more variables and pitfalls than the summer.

You may wonder why your score is worse even though the weather conditions are better than in summer. You need to examine the reasons for this. You can play better golf on moist ground rather than on dry ground, because your club passes through without effort.

In autumn it rarely rains, the ground is dry, sand is scattered to protect the grass, and the grass is not mown. The conditions of the ground in autumn are worse than those in summer.

There are many difficulties in autumn, such as the greens running too quickly, and the irregular running of the ball due to scattered sand. These difficulties can cause successive missed shots, in spite of the good weather and conditions. Stress can result.

Amateurs can often not understand how they have lost the sense of shots they had only a few weeks ago. They lose their sense of shots because of the changed conditions of the fairway, for which they have failed to account. Amateurs should try to understand the seasonal conditions and enjoy the golf in any case.

4) Winter

Since it is cold in the morning in late autumn, you should wear a vest or a sweater. In late November, it's difficult to tell if it is winter or autumn. A good swing is not possible if you are shivering from the cold!

In the colder months, green keepers may scatter sand on the fairways to protect the grass. The ground may become harder and the grass shorter—this makes your swing all the more difficult.

The grass should be in good shape for you to stretch your club, fully following the ball. If there is little grass, the club may be caught on the ground. Therefore, it is very difficult to swing straight because you often try to hit the ball harder to compensate for the resistance of the ground. It is fathomable that the condition of the grass can account for a difference of four or five points on your scorecard.

In mid-winter, golf may become easier than in the early winter. You will be wearing thick clothes, the ball runs well, and the club passes through the grass better. The ball flies farther and runs well on the green, and you can enjoy golf more. There is nothing that can quite compare with playing golf under a sprinkle of gentle snowflakes!

When you finish a round in the unbearable cold (minus 15 degrees on a windy day), you will enjoy a sense of accomplishment. Winter golf can be very interesting at times.

Winter is a season in which it is preferable to run the ball anywhere on the fairway or around the green. The sliced ball often bounces from the right wall to the left O.B, and a slightly sliced ball can touch the fairway but run out to O.B. Do not get too angry if you make an O.B. You can always excuse yourself by saying, "Winter golf is like that." You should get less stressed in winter. Golf is not easy. When it starts snowing in the middle of a round, sometimes you might just be satisfied with the beautiful snow around you while returning to the clubhouse.

Winter is also the season of hope: take the opportunity to practice a lot to beat your nemesis in the spring.

Let's all become players who can enjoy golf in all conditions of nature!

Part 11.

MIND CONTROL AND GOLF

AMATEUR

<<< GOLF

1. Golf and the Mind

People are born with both good and evil inside. We cry at birth. We start to smile as an infant, and learn little by little as we grow older. Our minds become complex. There are so many things to learn and do.

We learn gradually, and our mind constantly changes during the process of learning. In order to learn and do the right thing by ourselves, we Koreans try to learn the "Tao" (the Way) while we are still young.

No one can walk before crawling, or run before walking. We cultivate our mind and our behavior step by step. Similarly, we grow in various ways as golfers. We regret and correct any mistakes we have made.

When six to nine year old children start learning golf, they should do pretty much as they are taught. They understand the sense of golf in, or even before, one month of training. They tell you they don't know why their strokes were so bad yesterday. All beginners feel the same frustrations, and envy the good players. However, good golfers complain too. They also say they don't know why their game is off. Even professionals, including champion Tiger Woods, do not always feel comfortable with their play.

Player with a negative mind   Player with a positive mind

When you stand at the tee ground, your mind is often uneasy. Many times you might become angry after a stroke. From children to grown-ups, amateurs to professionals, everyone's golf and mind fluctuates. However, your mind should not become too excited, too stiff, too cocky, nor too fearful when you play golf.

In order to play better golf, you must be able to control your mind. Be calm and you will be able to translate your good intentions into good actions. We need to learn how to control our minds and cope with any situation that arises on the golf course.

2. Desirable Mindset at the Driving Range

Your play on any particular day depends on the rhythm and condition of your body at that point in time.

You feel good if your play is good. Some players even think of quitting golf altogether when they can't play well, thinking, "I don't have the aptitude needed for golf." Some people are quick to get angry, before they have the chance to analyze the causes of their flawed stroke-making.

As the body has a rhythm, so too does golf. It is a characteristic of amateur golf that its participants often fluctuate between good and poor play.

If you continue practicing for at least three years, in spite of the standard of your game, you will get to know yourself and you will begin to master your feelings.

Firstly, you should maintain a positive mindset while learning golf. Research how to play golf well, while watching the professionals play.

Secondly, regard practice as real play. Think carefully about every shot. When you miss a shot, calmly analyze the reasons why.

Thirdly, try to behave well in front of others. Cultivate the habit of praising others' play so as to always maintain a composed and generous attitude.

Fourthly, listen to the comments of other golfers. Accept good advice. Discard poor advice. Do not be too stubborn.

Tidbits of Information

★☆★ **Proverbs of golf (1)**

1) To ask is a shame for the moment, but not to ask is the shame of a lifetime.
   - An attitude of continuous learning is required.

2) Even fertile land gets weedy if not cultivated.
   -Even good players should practice constantly.

3) Courtesy begets courtesy.
   -If you behave politely to others, they will in turn behave politely to you.

4) Ten intellectuals cannot defeat one man of experience.
   - No one can beat a golfer who practices endlessly.

Part 12.

COMMON SENSE ON THE GOLF COURSE

1. Dressing for Golf

Golf wear is the fashion of nature. Golfers do not like wearing the same clothes as other players. They like to choose unique designs and colors. If you look at each professional player in a tournament, it is difficult to find any two players wearing the same clothes. This illustrates that players pay close attention to what they wear on the golf course.

As for the colors of golf wear, bright and clear colors are preferable to soft colors. In spring and summer, greenish colors matching the grass and trees are not recommended, because the team playing ahead should stand out so that those behind them can easily see them. In autumn, it is best to avoid colors too similar to red leaves or dead grass.

Sometimes it is difficult to find the time to keep our sports wear clean. But if you wear dirty or un-ironed clothes on the golf course, you will not be presenting yourself in the best light possible.

We all acknowledge that a player's golf wear reflects their handicap, and it is courteous to be clean and neat. In our social lives, one's clothes indicate our standard of living. On the golf course this is even more important.

"Neat clothes will put your mind in order, and an orderly mind will help you play stable golf that day."

2. Golf Etiquette

1) Keeping the Time: Keeping time is a strict rule of golf. Tee-off time must be kept and never delayed. If one player among four arrives late, the other three will get anxious. Therefore, you should arrive early at the golf club, and have a cup of tea to warm up your body. When I was a beginner, one of my four friends came late by 15 minutes. One single digit-handicap player told him that he had wasted 45 minutes, since each of the other three waited 15 minutes. My tardy friend was so sorry that he did not know what to say. Always bear in mind that time in golf is very important.

2) Dress etiquette: As mentioned above, golf is a gentleman's sport. Therefore, it is the etiquette of golf to dress smartly, like a gentleman, in accordance with club regulations. If you wear wrinkled clothes or unwashed trousers, other players may

look at you with suspicion. Conspicuous primary colors are recommended. A player who doesn't wear a hat does not give a good impression to others. Some golf courses require players to wear a formal suit to enter the golf club. In Korea, wearing short trousers in summer is not allowed. Long stockings are not banned, but few players wear them these days.

3) Teeing Ground: **Only one player at a time can step onto the teeing ground. The other players should stand back and keep quiet when a player is making a shot.**

4) Through the Green: **For Through the Green, you should hit the ball as it is, from the farthest ball to the nearest. You should quietly wait your turn. When another player is about to play, you should not practice a free swing or stand right behind them. If you don't know the rules, ask your caddy. Moreover, you should not waste too much time. Do not delay a game for more than five minutes looking for a lost ball.**

5) Green Edge: **On the edge of a green, the player whose ball is the farthest from the flag should play first. You should not practice when another player is about to play, nor play your ball while others are playing.**

6) On the Green: **When you have to putt after another player, you should always mark the spot before picking up the ball. You should keep quiet when another player is about to putt, and not stay on the left or right of the player. Ensure that your shadow does not appear in the ball's path. When you mark the ball, resist the temptation to mark a little forward of the ball, or secretly push the ball nearer to the hole. If you were to add up the distances made by golfers trying to sneak closer to the hole, it would travel around the globe many times! But it does the game no good whatsoever.**

7) Honors etiquette: **Know who the owner is. Do not automatically play first if you made a par on the previous hole.** The owner of the previous hole may also have made a par. It is safer to ask before playing, to avoid embarrassment.

8) Ambiguous shot: **If there is an ambiguity as to whether or not someone else's a shot was Out of Bounds an impolite player may say, "It was Out of Bounds, Make another shot" or, "I think it is still alive. If you are not sure, play a provisional ball."** This is poor sportsmanship. Avoid it wherever possible.

9) Etiquettes in hazards or bunkers: **Behavior such as looking at a person playing in a bunker or hazard, or watching closely to see whether the club touches the ground in a hazard, places undue pressure on the player making the shot. On the other hand, your club should not touch the ground in a bunker or hazard.**

10) Etiquette of betting: **Betting should be fair and clean. If you are too narrow-minded and tend to hurt other players' feelings, you will spoil the round. Avoid making cynical remarks of others' errors, or behaving in an unpleasant manner. Even when betting, behave like a gentleman—after all, you are playing the gentleman's sport. Cheating on your scorecard will only cause a quarrel.**

11) Etiquette of rules: **It is a poor idea to insist on the validity of your point unless you fully understand the rules. Even if you know the rules, it is polite to defer to another player if he insists too strongly. For players still in the learning process, many ambiguous situations can arise. In these cases, try to understand the other player's point of view. Do not give the other player a hard time over his mistake. A mis-ruling will not end the world. It is not wise to act foolishly and lose friends.**

Thoughtful consideration is required when applying the rules.

12) Score: Amateur golfers' scores are always entered lower on the scorecard than the actual scores. The reason is because, for example, the caddy writes a triple for a double par. The player himself remonstrates, and the caddy will correct the entry. Players may then take advantage of their caddy's preparedness to change the scores. It is said that amateurs place too much emphasis on the result. They are obsessed about trying to play a par, or a bogey at least. They cling to the results to such an extent that they often miss shots. Some golfers find joy in having their scores recorded lower than their actual result. Scores such as 144 or 150 cannot be found on an amateur's scorecard! They are mostly lower than 120 and often just over 100. Try to jot down your scores accurately as you play, and see the results. Some will be as high as 140. It is understandable for beginners to write lower than actual scores, but it is not polite for experienced players to do that.

13) Unsolicited lessons: It is a common practice for single digit-handicap players to offer tips on the course. However, they need to know whether or not the intended recipient wants a lesson before offering it. You, as an amateur, may be polite and answer, "Oh, yes" because you know they are good players. However, if they give you a tip when you are about to make a tee shot, it could be annoying. It is acceptable for players to offer tips when asked, but it becomes irritating if they interfere with another's play too often. This is often the cause of a golf course quarrel between husband and wife!

3. Psychology in Field

1) After scoring a series of pars, you may say to yourself, "Shall I make the best score today?" Your play will collapse from that moment.

2) "I don't remember the last time I practiced. I just brought my rusty old clubs with me." Nobody admits to having practiced a lot. The above comment suggests a lack of confidence.

3) "You play very well despite your inexperience." "Something is not right today." I did so well just a few days ago!" That's golf!

4) "I drank too much last night. My play is the worst today!" You can play well even after you drank alcohol. Anticipating that your play will suffer is your real problem.

5) "If only I was as young as you are! My driving distance is getting shorter and shorter." "A few years are not much difference. I can play farther now than last year!" Always thinking that you are old is the real reason you cannot drive the long distances you used to.

6) "I practiced a lot yesterday. Why is my play so bad?"
The reason that students ruin their exams despite plenty of study is because they crammed. Cramming does not work for golf either.

7) "They make lots of Out of Bounds's here. Be careful!"
This friend of yours is hoping that you will miss this shot!

Part 13.

THE BASIC RULES OF GOLF

AMATEUR
<<< GOLF

1. Teeing Ground

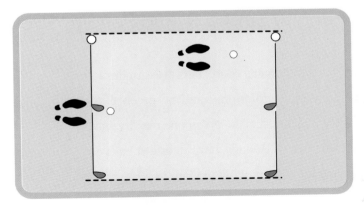

Choose a spot within two clubs of the tee-up position.

2. Who Goes First?

1) Farthest from the flag

For all shots other than the driver, the player whose ball is farthest from the flag shall play first. This rule applies to approaches as well as putting.

2) Balls stuck in the ground or floating on water

You may pick up a ball stuck in the ground on the fairway and drop it on the ground. You must not drop it nearer to the hole from its original position. If the ball falls in water formed after rain on the fairway, you may drop the ball no nearer the hole without penalty.

3) Advice

If you exchange advice during play, you shall get two penalty strokes. Golf is half in the thinking—players must do this themselves. However, it is all right to discuss announcements or rules.

3. One-Penalty Stroke & Two-Penalty Strokes

Golf is called the gentleman's sport. This also applies to penalty rules. Ungentlemanly behavior and intentional violations shall be given two penalty shots. Unintentional violations by force majeure shall be given one penalty shot.

More specifically, Out of Bounds, hazard, or lost balls are given only one penalty shot. Intentionally changing a lie, moving the ball to a superior place, or touching the ground with the club in a hazard, attract two penalty shots. Since a bunker is also a hazard, you are not permitted to touch the bunker ground with your club. If you do, two penalty shots shall be imposed.

4. Meters and Yards

Meters and yards are confusing. Some golf clubs use meters and others use yards. It is easy to wrongly use the same club for the same numbers of meters and yards.

Some golf clubs indicate distances in meters, but they appear shorter than yards! It seems that each golf club has different standards of distance. On a certain golf course that uses the yard system, you cannot make the distance even if you calculated it in meters! On another golf course, the distance in meters seems the same as in yards!

I believe they should standardize the indications – either yards or meters. Until they do, however, amateur golfers don't have a choice but to consult the caddy about the distances.

5. Dropping of the Ball: 1-club vs 2-club

There are two cases of drops: a no-penalty drop and a penalty drop.

When you drop with a penalty, you may drop the ball within two club lengths of its original position. When you drop without penalty, you may drop the ball within one club length of its original position.

For free drop areas set by local rules, manhole covers, sprinkler heads, and immovable obstacles (such as props for newly planted trees) you may drop the ball within one club length of its original position.

When your ball falls in a lateral water hazard, or when an unplayable ball is announced, you receive one penalty shot, and you may drop the ball within two club lengths of its original position.

6. Out of Bounds

O.B. stands for Out of Bounds. This means that the ball went off the fairway, as indicated by white poles. When you hit a ball O.B., one penalty shot is imposed, and you should replay the shot from the same position your O.B. shot was made from.

Debates on O.B. areas always occur between amateurs. They will often insist that the ball is "right on the O.B. line." Kind friends or unfamiliar companions may acknowledge your assertion, but your close friends, or those who have a strong desire to win, may not easily relent.

If the ball is on the inner line of the white poles, it is not O.B. If it is on the middle or outer lines of the white poles, it is O.B. Since there is no judge in an amateurs' game, the etiquette of golf suggests you should settle disputes by mutual concessions.

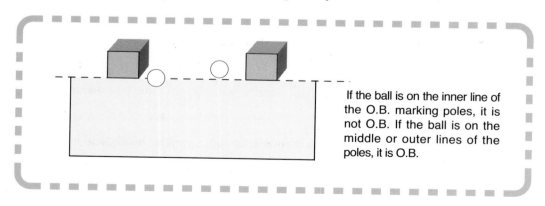

If the ball is on the inner line of the O.B. marking poles, it is not O.B. If the ball is on the middle or outer lines of the poles, it is O.B.

7. Ball Under a Tree

If an unplayable ball is announced, one penalty shot is imposed, and you should drop the ball within two clubs length of the ball's original position.

8. Ball on a Sprinkler Head

If the ball falls on a sprinkler head, you can drop the ball within one club length of its original position without penalty.

9. Ball Under the Props for a Tree

When the ball falls under the props for a tree, you can drop the ball within one club length from its original position without penalty.

10. Loose Impediment

You are allowed to move leaves or stones out of the way.

Part 14.

PUTTING BASICS

1. Ball Marking

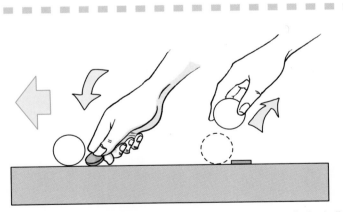

Mark the ball on the green and then pick up the ball. If you touch the ball while marking its position, two penalty shots will be imposed.

2. Shadow

Do not cross the path of another player's ball with your shadow. This is poor golf etiquette.

3. Ball Placement

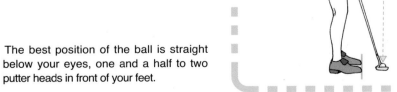

The best position of the ball is straight below your eyes, one and a half to two putter heads in front of your feet.

4. Swing Arcs of Short and Long Putts

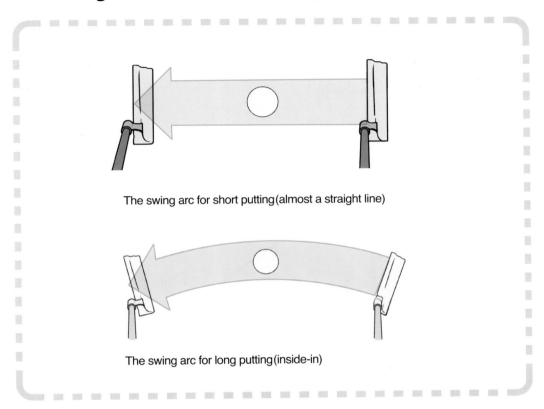

The swing arc for short putting(almost a straight line)

The swing arc for long putting(inside-in)

5. Pro Side and Amateur Side

There is an old saying, "Never Up, Never In." This means that to succeed in putting, you should hit the ball strongly enough for the ball to pass the hole. Similarly, when you make your putt on a downward slope from the side, you should hit the ball 'above the hole.' If you send the ball 'below the hole,' the probability of success is less than one percent. The putting line stretching to 'above the hole' is called the pro's side, and the putting line stretching to 'below the hole' is called the amateur's side.

The lack of boldness to hit the ball above the hole on such a slope seems one of the weaknesses of amateur golfers. Putt the ball strongly enough to pass the hole by 20cm, and always, aim above the hole cup.

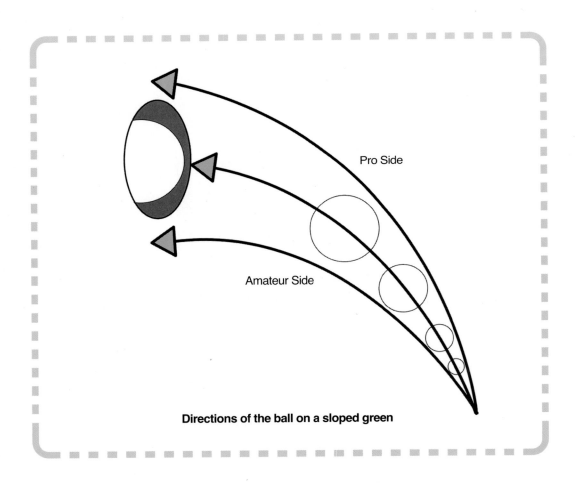

Pro Side

Amateur Side

Directions of the ball on a sloped green

Part 15

GOLF CLUB BASICS

AMATURE
<<< GOLF

1. Basic Knowledge

1) Selecting Clubs

If your clubs do not suit your physical strength and features, it will take much longer for you to master golf, no matter how expensive your clubs are. Beginners need clubs they can swing easily, smoothly, and rhythmically. There are three factors involved in the selection of golf clubs.

① The length and weight of the club

The longer and heavier a club is, the faster the speed of the head at the point of impact. Longer and heavier clubs can hit the ball farther. They do, however, require greater physical strength and an advanced technique. Since beginners or physically weaker people are unlikely to be able to form a correct swing with such clubs, it is wiser for them to choose clubs that are shorter and easier to swing.

② The hardness of the shaft

The hardness of the middle of the shaft is indicated on the club. For strong and skilled players, a long, hard shaft with a heavy head is the optimal type of club. Physically weaker golfers and beginners should choose softer and lighter clubs with elastic shafts. By using the elasticity of the shaft, the ball can be hit farther with less effort.

★ Indications of hardness of the shaft:
  - Ladies (L) : appropriate for females, seniors, and weaker males.
  - Average (A) : appropriate for strong females and weaker males.
  - Regular (R) : appropriate for female professionals and most males.
  - Stiff (S) : a hard shaft appropriate for strong males.
  - Extra Stiff (X) : the hardest shaft, appropriate only for professionals.

③ Swing weight

The swing weight (the weight you feel when swinging) is an approximation used so that players may use clubs of an appropriate weight. Having a sense of the head weight will help you to find the swing weight.

There are two kinds of club weight: the weight you feel when you hold a club, and the weight you feel when you swing a club. It is very important to choose clubs of the right weights for you.

The swing weight indicates the balance of weight in the club between the head end of the club and the grip end. When you put a club on your fingers, the closer the center of weight is to the head end of the club, the heavier the head end is, (and the lighter the grip end of the club is.) Irrespective of the club's weight, this relative weight balance makes a great deal of difference between whether the weight of the head feels light or heavy.

Swing weight is indicated in five levels: A, B, C, D, and E. Each level is divided again into 10 sublevels from 0 to 9. The difference between any two subsequent sublevels is about two grams.

- A0 - B9: appropriate for boys, girls, and the elderly.
- C0 - C7: appropriate for females and weaker males.
- C8 - D3: appropriate for most males.
- D4 - D9: appropriate for stronger males and professionals.
- E: appropriate for professionals and the strongest hitters (rarely used in Korea).

2. Forged and Cast Irons

How do they make iron heads? It may help you understand the characteristics of your clubs if you understand the process of manufacturing forged and cast irons.

1) The manufacturing of forged irons

Forged irons are made from heated round iron poles. These iron poles are refined in advance, so that the direction of their inner metal texture is identical to that of the longitudinal direction of the iron poles. The metal texture maintains its direction even under extreme duress, such as if the iron poles are tampered with, or if their shapes are changed. After undergoing many stages of forging, the texture gradually becomes finer and stronger due to the internal cohesion of metals. This results in a soft metal of high quality processing.

Forged iron is much more solid and stable than cast iron. It is what gives golfers that good feeling when they hit the golf ball. Compare these two illustrative scenarios. Imagine making a baseball bat by cutting wood from a tree, and gently shaving it in the direction of the texture. You then make another by gluing sawdust together with adhesive, and compression-molding it. Anyone will tell you which feels better.

● The Manufacturing Process: An iron bar is struck with a hammer to shape it into its desired form. An iron-head shaped stamper, and a high-pressure press are used to stamp the head into an increasingly precise shape. A skilled craftsman then polishes it.

2) The manufacturing of cast irons

A cast iron is made from completely melted iron. There is no metal texture. The molten metal is poured into a mold and hardened. It does not have a fixed structure. As a result, some parts may have hollow points inside, and these clubs tend to be broken easily.

★ Lost Wax Process Manufacturing

① Put wax in a mold.

② Remove the hardened wax.

③ Make an inlet in the hardened wax. Connect the many pieces of wax together in the shape of a branch with leaves.

④ Soak them in water and clay mix for ceramic ware.

⑤ Bury the bundle of wax, and mix it in sand that is capable of withstanding heat. Repeat steps four and five until a clam-shape is formed.

⑥ Apply heat to melt the wax in the clam-shaped mold. Heat it in a gas fire furnace to completely melt the remaining wax.

⑦ Pour molten iron into the space from which the wax was removed.

⑧ Remove the clam-shaped mold from the inlet for molten iron.

⑨ Cut it from the trunk and break the sand mold. Polish it.

⑩ Production is now completed.

As described above, low cost mass production of cast iron is possible in precise shapes using metallic patterns because no additional work is required for the finishing process.

3. Flex

The players who use a hard shaft inappropriately can increase their flying distance by switching to a softer shaft.

A softer shaft not only flies a ball higher, but also offers effects such as longer distances and a good feel. A soft shaft bends during the down swing, and straightens at impact to deliver more swing energy. This "kick" effect results in the ball flying further.

However, improving the feeling of the swing must be secondary to achieving longer distances when choosing the flex. Bear in mind that too soft a shaft will decrease your accuracy.

As most golfers place more emphasis on distance and a better feel than on accuracy, it is preferable to select the softest shaft you can possibly control within the limits of your recommended swing speed. If you have a choice between two shafts of different strengths within the overlapping ranges of your recommended swing speed, you should choose a strong shaft for higher accuracy and a soft shaft for greater speed.

4. Torque

The torque of the shaft is the extent to which the shaft can withstand twisting strength. The lower the torque, the more the shaft can withstand twisting strength. In general, four or lower is considered a low torque, while five or higher is considered a high torque. The higher the torque, the more susceptible to twisting is the club.

However, the difference between high and low torque shafts is not as great as you may imagine. For example, the torque of a steel shaft will be between 4.0 and 4.3. The torque of a graphite shaft has a wider range of torque: from 1.6 to 8. The torque of the shaft affects accuracy and, to a certain degree, the feeling.

A lower torque feels harder, and prevents the club head from turning in the process of the down swing. On the other hand, a higher torque feels softer. If the difference of torque between two shafts with the same flex is two or greater, even amateurs can feel the difference.

You may use a shaft with high torque to improve the feel of your strokes. However, for golfers who have a fast tempo that accelerates during the down swing, low torque shafts may decrease their accuracy because the club's face may turn during the down swing, preventing them from making accurate impact.

The torque affects the five characteristics of distance, accuracy, trajectory, feel, and back spin considerably, although not absolutely. Too low a torque does not aid distance and trajectory, but greatly affects accuracy and feeling.

5. Bend Point

A bend point refers to the part of the shaft that bends the most when force is applied. However, a more accurate definition describes the bend 'point' as the distribution of bending in the entire shaft.

The bend point will be indicated as low bend, mid bend, or high bend. On a low-bend shaft, the grip end is hard and the head end is soft. On a mid-bend shaft, both the grip and the head end of the club have some degree of hardness. On a high-bend shaft, the grip end is soft and the head end is hard.

However, the actual differences in centimeters are not large. The distance between low bend and high bend on a shaft is only 5cm or less, and it is always located near the center of the shaft. The bend point of a shaft has considerable influence on the feeling of the shot, but little influence on the trajectory of the ball. Therefore, it is natural that you should put emphasis on its influence to the feeling of the shot when selecting the bend point of a shaft. You can even amplify the "kicking" effect at impact, by playing with a low-bend shaft in which the head end side is soft.

Some manufacturers exaggerate the "kicking" effect, and use the term "kick point" instead of bend point. This may work in marketing terms but it is a flawed technical concept. A kick point also refers to the part of the shaft that bends the most, whereas a bend point measures the degree of bending under force from both sides of a shaft. A kick point is measured by applying force only from the head end of the club.

Many people believe that the bend point determines the trajectory of ball. This is an overestimation of the influence the bend point has. In fact, the overall flex of a shaft has much greater influence on the trajectory of the ball. Therefore, if you would like to change the trajectory of the ball, you should take flex into consideration. If you desire a high trajectory of flight, choose a soft shaft with a low bend. If you desire a low trajectory, choose a hard shaft with a high bend.

The bend point has enormous influence on the feel of the stroke. Since a low-bend shaft gives a softer feeling than a high-bend shaft, you should choose a low-bend shaft if you are the kind of golfer who seeks satisfaction from the feel of your strokes.

6. Balance Point

The balance point refers to the center of weight on a shaft. It is the balance point of weight when you hold a shaft horizontally. A balance point is classified into low balance, mid balance, and high balance. On a low-balance shaft, the tip of the head is heavier, while on a high-balance shaft, the butt of the grip is heavier. Although a lower balance point creates increased swing weight because the head end of the club is heavier, it does not have a large influence on accuracy. For example, if you lower the swing weight by reducing the weight of the shaft from 120g to 85g, you can use a low-balance shaft to compensate the swing weight to a considerable degree, without changing the weight of the head.

7. Distance of Driver Shot by Swing Speed

Swing Speed (mph)	80	85	90	95	100	105	110	115	120	125	130
Pure Distance (yards)	146	169	187	208	225	241	256	269	281	292	302
Initial Ball Speed (mph)	113	120	127	134	141	148	155	162	169	176	183
Initial Spin (rpm)	2256	2397	2538	2679	2820	2961	3102	3243	3384	3525	3666
Duration of Flight (sec)	3.8	4.3	4.8	5.3	5.8	6.2	6.7	7.1	7.5	7.8	8.2

The above numbers were acquired using a driver with a head weight of 198g and a loft of 10 degrees. The pure distance (carry only, excluding run) was determined by each swing speed.

PGA pros have a swing speed of about 120 miles per hour, and reach an average carry only distance of 280 yards. For example, Tiger Woods has a swing speed of 130 mph, and uses a Titlist 975D driver of 7.5 degrees, with a head weight of 204g. If you calculate the expected distance with these data, you get 297 yards. In fact, he recorded an average of about 289 yards during the tour in 1999, and 297 yards in 2000.

★☆★ **Truths about golf from the amateur's viewpoint (1)**

1) It is difficult to play golf well, but it can be fun even when you don't.

2) Children can play better than adults.

3) It is easy to cheat, but you will regret it later.

4) Golf bring both hope and despair.

5) If you are afraid to choose a difficult club boldly, bear in mind that you cannot use the club forever.

6) Watching a great swing does you no good unless you can apply it to yours.

7) Everybody swears at themselves on the golf course.

8) 10 Ph.D degrees are of no use on the golf course.

9) Golf is more enjoyable than sex. You never grow tired of it!

10) You should play with courtesy on the golf course, even as you go back and forth between heaven & hell.

Part 16

STORIES OF MY FELLOW GOLFERS

1. Four Mountains and Golf

By Seok San Cho Seok Man

★ First Story

San is the Korean for mountain and Sa means four. It has been a long time since I explained to anyone these nicknames. Four mountains is the title of a traditional Korean story.

I have some good friends who I have known for several decades. We all used to have our own hobbies, but have become very close after enjoying golf together. We used to meet for a drink occasionally and golf gave us a decent excuse.

One day after drinking I bestowed pseudonyms to each of my old playmates. One friend whose surname is Song, I named 'Song san'. Another friend's surname is Chung, so he became 'Chung San'. Seok is my name so I became 'Seok San'. Lastly a friend who lives in Ilsan became 'Il san'. Since then we have been collectively known as 'Sa San', the four mountains. When we are together we pretend that we are noblemen with refined tastes, so intoxicating are our pseudonyms.

'How are you, Chung San?'
'Ah, Seok San! How have you been?'

When I call then at home it can lead to confusion···

'Oh hello, may I talk to Il San?'
'Who is Il San?'
'That is your husbands nickname!'
'Hahaha, how obnoxious!'

We like our pseudonyms because they are fun and easy to remember. All of us are

---

★ ☆ ★ **Meaning of Four Mountains**

It is a Korean custom to give a nickname or second name to friends, which symbolizes their character or activities. Four nicknames and their meanings are summarized below:

Songsan (Pine tree Mountain) signifies his will to always maintain a firm spirit and stay green.

Cheongsan (Green Mountain) signifies that he is like a mountain that is always fresh and green.

Ilsan (One Mountain) was named because this friend lives in Ilsan.

Seoksan (Stone Mountain) signifies that he is very strong like a stone mountain.

over 60 years old so it is easier than using formal titles, they sound elegant to others, and the only problem is that they were self-imposed.

★ Second Story

I experienced a funny episode when calling my friend 'Song San' who owns a construction company.

'Hello. This is 'X' construction company' the secretary answered.

'Hi, may I speak to President Song?'

'He is not in the office. Shall I leave a message?'

'Please ask him to call Seok San'

The next day the secretary informed the president⋯

'Mr. President, you need to call Seok San'

'Hmm, which Seok San?'

'He just said Seok San'

'Ahh, that fellow, ha ha ha!'

The secretary slanted her head and looked confused. Unexpectedly I had become an aggregate company!

★ Third Story

There are unwritten rules for golf rounds that have been maintained for a long time among the Sa San. Since we are all bogey players, the same handicap is applied among us. If one of us scores mid 80's, he becomes the day's winner. I used to win many of the games for a long time, but I have not won in the past year. It's not that their golf has improved, but that my handicap kept rising. If you win a game, you are entitled to be treated as a respected older brother, and addressed as "boss" or "big brother" by the other three for a month. You are treated as if you have been promoted from a colonel to a general.

Firstly, the others must reply to your call with, "Yes, big brother," or, "I will do as you say." No one may disobey your orders for a month. They have no choice but to show respect to you in any event.

"welcome, boss?"

Secondly, the others should open car doors for you. You may want to wait at the car until the "little brothers" appear and some pretty lady passes by. It will taste bitter for the others, but your right to the tyranny of the winner is maintained for the whole month. We never violated this hard rule of the jungle, because we were all fearful of the boomerang effect in the event that we were on the receiving end.

However, it is not always a one-way street. A big brother has responsibilities and duties. Firstly, when you become the big brother, you must treat your younger brothers to lunch or dinner.

"Is this Seok San? This is your big brother."

"Ah, big brother, what is the occasion?"

"What do you say to having dinner tomorrow?"

"Ah, yes, I will call the other brothers."

It is like a boss and his followers of a club.

Thirdly, the big brother has to arrange the time and place for the next golf game, thereafter notifying the younger brothers.

"Ah, Il San? This is your big brother."

"Yes, big brother. How are you, Sir?"

"We will meet next Wednesday at ABC Country Club. Is there any problem?"

"Absolutely, not. I will be there."

In this manner, all of us are on the lookout for the chance to acquire sovereignty every month. We tell dirty joke and use bad language all the time during the 18 holes—but we never get angry at each other, or offend any young caddies.

This is the joy of golf that I wouldn't forego for anything else.

These golf buddies make my life more valuable.

2. I Went To Put Up My Hair Only to Come Back With My Head Down

"I had delusions of grandeur"

By Gang Hyeon Sik

My golf career is only a year old, but I have already had my share of experiences. At first, I started playing golf to build business relationships. I since fell in love with the game!

Before I took up golf, I didn't understand why so many people were crazy about it. It seemed to me like a simple, basic game. How wrong I was!

I have changed my clubs five times, and my driver three times since I first learned golf. Too often? Maybe. But I don't always get new clubs. At first, I practiced for two months with Taylor Made irons. I then went to Philos golf course to put up my hair (a Korean phrase meaning to do something for the first time) with a professional golfer friend of mine. I came back with my head down in shame. I thought golf was very difficult. Nevertheless, I was not discouraged and regarded it as a blessing that I found golf to be so difficult, because I enjoy challenging myself. Easy is not fun. I practiced with great vigor.

> ★☆★ **Raise hair**
> It is an old Korean custom for maidens to grow their hair and tie it with a pigtail ribbon. When they get married they should raise their hair and tie it over their head, which indicates that they are not a maiden any more. As a figure of speech, we say someone has "raised their hair" when they go to golf for the first time after learning golf.

One day, my brother-in-law, hearing that I began playing golf, presented me with a Bridgestone X-5000 Life Shaft. I was so happy that I practiced a great deal. It became a routine drill for me to swing with a driver, irons, and a putter for two to three hours a day. I found that my golf was improving faster than other people's. I was full of confidence and went to the Libera Golf Club for a round. I made a good driver shot and a good second shot. The ball fell in front of the green. Now I had to make an approach. I ended up just wandering around, experiencing what they call, "cold water, warm water." The caddy watching me said, "I thought you were a single digit-handicap player when I saw you play the first two shots. I am worried that you will have a hard time today." She had thought that I must have been a good player because my irons were the type used by many single digit-handicap players.

I then switched to Mizuno S10 clubs, which were popular among Japanese pros. A senior of mine, with whom I often play golf with, used the clubs and played so well, scoring in the 70's. I was so eager to play well. My fellow players told me they were difficult to play with and tried to dissuade me from buying these clubs. But I wanted to improve by practicing with difficult clubs. One day, I went for a round in Giheung with my new clubs. The caddy, seeing my clubs, commented, "If you can't score below 85 with them, you should throw them away." My play was ruined because I felt the burden of my new clubs. After that incident, I changed to Mizuno SV30, the newest model. Although they were for advanced golfers, they felt far easier to handle compared with the Mizuno S10 clubs. Less than two weeks later, I had to replace them with Bridgestone TS 201clubs! I also changed my driver from the Mizuno SII 300 to the Bridgestone RV 10. I changed my putters twice. Did I become a good player as a result of changing my clubs?

I realized that becoming a good golfer depends on one's inborn talent and on practice. I intend to use my current irons until they are worn and can no longer be used. I feel ashamed that I blamed my clubs when I should have blamed myself during the past year. I will practice hard to score in the 70's. Golf can be a fight with one's self.

3. Management Skills Learned from Golf

By Song Hee Nam

Like many people in Korea, I first became interested in golf when Seri Pak dramatically won the US Women's Open after a close match that extended to extra holes in 1998. Her victory was especially touching, as it came at a time when our country was in the grip of financial crisis.

At the time, my brother presented some golf clubs to me, saying, "A top manager like you will benefit in life by learning golf for self control." After some hesitation, I stopped at a bookstore, bought a golf instruction book for beginners, and began learning about gripping, addressing, and aiming (alignment and targeting).

Thinking I had learned enough of the basics, I went to a nearby driving range. I couldn't even hit a ball! That was four years ago. Now, I am an ordinary golfer who can mingle with fellow golfers without much difficulty. I play with consideration for others, and regard self-control as the most important thing in a golf player. Although my golf is not as good as some of my peers, I am very popular among them because I emphasize manners and try to make them feel comfortable. When I play golf, I do my best on each hole, while complying strictly with the rules of golf. I compare the game of golf with business. I pledge to myself to relax (emphasis on substantiality), and not head up (treading the path of management). When I compare golf with management, I can see that all kinds of business difficulties are caused by being too tense, sidetracking, and neglecting research and development.

I tell myself, "Don't be greedy. Just watch the ball" when I'm at the tee shot of the first hole. I play my best shots only when I can differentiate between the holes that I should play boldly, and those that I should play safely, using accurate diagnoses and analyses for each hole. Only this way will I have no regrets after I finish the 18 holes.

4. Fearless Beginner Couple

By Choi Bok Nam and Kim Wan Dong

In early October when the autumn season had just arrived, my husband and I boarded an airplane bound for Bangkok. We were full of anticipation and excitement - we were going on a golf tour. But then···

A call from the tour guide woke us up at dawn. We rushed to the golf course. As always, we staked our lives on wagers. Since it was hot, we drank our beers as if they were mineral water. We played two rounds of 18 holes intoxicated by the alcohol and the hot weather. The beginner couple we were with didn't know if we had come to play golf or collect stray balls.

The next day my husband prepared countless balls because he wanted to play each hole with several balls. But I held him back. As a result, he didn't play well, nor count his score. He got angry and became even hotter. We became very nervous about each stroke since money was at stake. We finished the game in a heated manner.

We returned to our hotel without saying a word to each other. Who said a quarrel between husband and wife was like cutting water with a knife? The day felt like it would never end. I regret that we had to fight when we were supposed to be enjoying our three-day stay in a foreign land··· We still continue to wager on golf games··· and we still quarrel on the golf course.

"Where are you going? One more game!"

5. Some Tips for Beginners

By Jeong Yeo Seon

I first learned to play golf about 3 years ago, but have been playing seriously for about 2 years. A friend of mine was a student of an Australian golf pro and he introduced me to the game. I am very athletic, so at first I advanced very quickly. I admit I became a little conceited. Unfortunately, for various reasons, I had to change my teachers five times and this weakened my style. I gradually lost interest in golf.

A year later I began playing again. The friend who first got me started had become and excellent player. However, I was not put off and continued playing even when my scores were terrible.

I would like to tell you a story about when I was playing golf at my golf club.
One Monday, during a golf lovers gathering, I played 18 holes in a hurry. I was playing atrociously, with many duff shots. I hit the ball with my 7 wood. As I watched the ball, I noticed something following it. I looked at my club, only to see the shaft remaining and I realized that it was my club head following the ball!

The caddie congratulated me, it was the first time she had ever seen this happen. I keep the club to this day without repair-ing it. It reminds me of my errors and to never play in such a hurry again.

The advice I wanted to share is the phrase, 'well begun is half done'.
Always lay a solid foundation in everything you do.

6. Well Begun is Half Done

By Park Chae Hoon

I started learning golf in February 2000. Almost three years have passed since then. I still remember the extremely cold winter when I first began playing golf.

Even though I couldn't even fully extend my fingers in the freezing cold, I was filled with excitement on my first trip to the golf course. Looking back, I don't know what I thought I was doing. But, if I had not behaved with such enthusiasm, I would not be scoring even close to 100 nowadays.

I was a sports fanatic. I was crazy about soccer before I took up golf. I found golf after searching for a sport that I could enjoy for a lifetime. Playing soccer was getting harder the older I got. I watched TV programs and read books on golf to prepare myself for it, and visited a driving range in February 2000 for the first time.

As they say, "Well begun is half done." In the beginning, things were very difficult for me. Blisters formed on my hands, and I couldn't extend the third finger of my left hand the next morning. When I first began learning golf, I was in the middle of a two month break before joining a new company. Therefore, I could practice all day long. After only 15 days, I went for a round on the Bal-An public golf course.

It was early morning and I could hardly see anything through the dense fog. I don't remember how I finished the nine holes. Since then, I have always frequented public golf courses early in the morning by myself. If I had to work at dawn, would I be quite so joyful? I wonder how I could hit so many balls all day long?

I still remember vividly the time when I made my first birdie in a beginners' competition organized by a certain golf club. It was a par-3 hole of 155 yards. The ball I hit with a # 7 iron flew to the left, luckily curved back to the right because of the wind, and fell near the hole cup. When I walked to the spot, I found the ball was on a downward incline about 1.2m away from the hole. I putt the ball lightly, looking at the hole-cup on my left. The ball ran straight into the hole-cup. It was the first birdie in my life! Since I was the only player who made a birdie that day, I received the birdie prize, and a pair of golf shoes as a gift.

Golf requires a great deal of patience. Golf seems easy when you play well, but it feels like the most difficult sport in the world when you play poorly. However, golf can be the most exciting and delightful sport, if you can forgo your greed and just enjoy it. It is also a sport that you can enjoy until you die. My handicap is still around 20, but I have already mastered a half of golf.

7. Sad Memory about Golf

By Bang Yeon Soon

I first started playing golf because it seemed like a cool and fun sport! I signed up at a driving range and began receiving lessons from KPGA Pro "General" Kim!

He was suffering from leukemia at the time but still gave me lessons at the driving range in the country from time to time. He was afraid of catching a cold, which could be fatal to him. His swing was so beautiful. His swing arc was so smooth and natural, but his impact so powerful that the ball flew in a very nice trajectory, just like his soul··· he is no longer with us. But I will always remember him.

I practiced eagerly because I fell in love with his swing. In springtime March, when everything was reviving, he passed away. I pray to God that he is no longer ill, and can play golf to his heart's content in heaven.

Golden colored grass, eleven golf clubs, and all the various kinds of balls···.

I can't help but love these things because of my teacher who is still in my heart.

8. Hey, Do Not Hurry

By Choi Jong In

You didn't work hard to sow seeds in spring.

Why do you try to harvest?

Take it easy and think of it as taking a walk with your friend.

The prairie, clean air, sun shine, and the promenade.

This is GOLF.

It took a lot of time and money to be here.

You may want to get what you paid for, but do not hurry.

Behave patiently and calmly. It is the way it should be.

How much did you hesitate before coming here?

Follow the little white ball, and you will soon regret the early sunset.

Now-do not tell me I'm crazy.

You want to play golf again and again because of this.

Ignorant people say it is extravagant.

You play on a prairie, and pay tax in ecstasy.

It is the destination terminal at the twilight of life.

9. I Learned Golf This Way

By Han Gwang Seong

Now you can learn golf from TV and the Internet. However, only 15 years ago, there was nothing to hold on to except the pros. Anyway, it is a good thing that we can learn golf through a variety of media.

However, you cannot play golf well just by receiving lessons. The key is how the process develops. For me, I learned the basics thoroughly for the first six months. I studied the grip, the address, stance, and other natural poses. I even practiced with my body tied by a waist belt, so that my arms would not move away from my body at impact.

Improve your golf just by watching!

I drew a back swing arc on the mirror in the veranda of my house. I concentrated on making a perfect circle. The poses that I learned during the first six months didn't change a bit until now. Every amateur should consider the first six months as the most important period. Thereafter, every thing will be OK.

10. Lightning

By Sylvia Taylor

One autumn my friends and I were playing at the golf club in a Medal rounding. The weather was very patchy but we continued to play. As we stood on the 18th green to putt out and I was just about to putt, a flash of lightening hit the fairway behind us followed by an Almighty Crash of Thunder, the greens shook, needless to say we snatched up our balls and fled.

As we were running through a torrent of rain towards the clubhouse, which overlooks the 18th green a loud strident voice rang out, "Ladies you have omitted to mark your balls!." It was the Lady Captain and she was incensed that we had ruined our rounding by not marking our balls and thus we were disqualified from the ladies competition. The thought that we may have been electrocuted did not seem to occur to her.

11. Golf and Modesty

By Ahn Byeong Ok

Everyone likes to boast about what he or she is good at. Even when someone talks in a modest way, if you listen carefully, it turns out often to be boastful. If there is one exception to this rule, it is golf.

I have enjoyed golf for almost 10 years now, but everyone says before a round, "I haven't practice lately," (more often than not, it means they have been sharpening their skills a lot!), or "My skills do not improve much these days." In fact, you can rest assured that these players have been playing better than their handicaps recently. Furthermore, when someone makes an O.B., they say, "You haven't warmed up yet. You seldom make an O.B., you know." This really means, "I'm so glad to see you make a mistake."

I have given a lot of thought to this phenomenon for some time. "Why are they so extremely modest in golf, unlike other sports or everyday life?" After my own analysis, I came to these conclusions:

① Some golfers are sincerely humble. (This is rare, though.)
② Insecure, golfers exaggerate their weaknesses. They are preparing in advance, because golf is unpredictable. If it works out better than you thought, you get praised; if not, you still lose nothing.
③ In a betting scenario, the winning strategy is often modesty.

This makes golf interesting. Even if your golf does not turn out as you wished, you can remind yourself of the saying, "My boring day might be the long tomorrow of the dead." Seize the day and practice hard.

12. Golf and Life

By Han Yang Hee

Golf is often likened to life—probably because both give unexpected surprises and frustrations.

10 years ago I first took up golf, playing mainly with a particular friend of mine. Even though we started at around the same time, her scores were in the 90's while mine were between 110 and

"What are you doing, mom?"

120. Since she didn't look like an athletic person, I was so annoyed after playing against her that I couldn't sleep well. I would think, "Ah, this must be the right swing!" and get up in the middle of night to practice. If someone saw me doing this with my disheveled hair, they may have thought I was crazy!

My husband would poke fun at me, saying, "Your friend has the talent for golf even though she may not do other things well. You have no talent for golf, even though you are good at other things." Despite such comments, I was determined to prove to them that I was a good golf player. I practiced my swing with anything I could find, from umbrellas to a rice scoop! Thanks to so much effort and after much trial and error, I jointly won the third prize at the Ceragem golf tournament the year before last. I will keep practicing and play as often as I can to maintain a high level of golf, even if it is a sport that can never be conquered.

13. From Beginner to Single Digit-Handicap Player

By Kim Seong Man

I started playing golf on April 2, 2000, purely to improve my business relationships. I tried my best to socialize with presidents of my client companies. Although most of them had played golf for 5 to 10 years, I thought I could catch up with them quickly if I practiced more than them.

I practiced for one hour in early mornings, one hour during the day, and one hour in the evenings for two months. I then went to the Incheon International Golf Club for my first round of golf. I was so happy to see the beautiful golf course – of which I had only heard. I wandered around not knowing where my ball was flying. I made a birdie at the 10th hole and scored 99!! A pro golfer bought me a drink that day. I was full of pride, and thought that golf was easy and that I would become a single digit-handicap player in no time at all.

As they say, your golf and your child are beyond your control. My scores didn't improve much since that first day. I scored 104, 108, 98, and 103 afterwards. I hated myself, but kept practicing with the belief that I would make it no matter what. I lost a lot of money betting, and I repeatedly felt defeated and angry.

Then, one day in April 2001, I made an eagle at the par-4 #10 hole at the Incheon International Golf Club. I was overjoyed and rolled around on the green. It cost me about 1,500 dollars for the drinks I bought others. Since then, I have been a bogey player with an average score of 90, and I have not lost much money from betting. I eagerly wanted to become a single digit-handicap player. While surfing around on the Internet, I found an amateur golf site and joined it in July 2001. It is a privilege to learn from other members.

At last, on September 30, 2001 at the Song Choo Country Club, I recorded a single score for the first time with 78. It is true that you can succeed if you learn earnestly and make continuous efforts. I have made 70's about 10 times since, while none of my peers has made a single score in their long golfing careers. Before, they betted with handicaps, but now they wouldn't bet unless I were given a handicap!

However, I always try to behave amiably and keep manners for business rather than winning a bet. Moreover, I have fallen in love with golf. I can exercise in the clean air. It is like killing two birds with one stone. I can never express my gratitude for the happiness golf has given to me. Even if I get irritated because of poor form, there is no greater happiness for me than playing golf. I can learn all the wisdom in the world by playing golf.

★☆★ Truths about golf from the amateur's viewpoint (2)

11) The good pro shows interest and trust to others.

12) "Become an honest duffer rather than a foul single digit-handicapper," said the famous Bob Jones. Those who maintain the humble minds of a beginner are better golfers than those who try to save their O.B. shots.

13) A soft swing begets a beautiful swing, and a beautiful swing makes the ball draw a beautiful curve to the target.

14) The best teaching method for juniors is to induce interest and competition.

15) The golf swing is like the path of a wise man. Golfers who take a byway, will end up looking for the broad way.

16) It is not good to diagnose a sick golfer as you like. Each golf doctor has a different opinion.

17) It is more comfortable to jot down your scores, rather than become suspicious about how the caddy wrote your scores.

18) If someone says, "I should play one provisional shot if it was O.B. - but I think it wasn' t," is he being honest with himself?

19) As you think, so is golf. It is like self-hypnotism.

20) Who will not be pleased to see other players' missed shots?

14. Who is the True Amateur Golfer?

By Park Seong Joon

I had my first opportunity to play golf in 1987 when many other professors changed their hobbies from tennis to golf. We signed up at a driving range near the hospital as a group. Many of them also bought memberships to a golf club, which was selling them at a discount. Two weeks after I took my golf lessons, I had to stop playing golf because my golf teacher moved to another golf club. The professor in charge of the general surgery department gave me strict orders to put my golf lessons on hold until I was 40.

I took up golf again in March 1991 at the recommendation of my senior professor. He said I had to learn golf before going to the USA in September that year as an exchange professor. For one month, I practiced a few hours every week day evening after finishing my round of patients on weekdays, and from 10 am to 10 pm on Sundays. I experienced all kinds of golfers' pains including trigger finger. I couldn't stretch my fingers in the morning and felt pain in my back, shoulders, wrists, and chest.

Thanks to these efforts, I was able to score 105 in my first round at the New Korea Country Club after three months. Fifteen days later, I had my second round at the Joong Boo Country Club with my fellow professors. They had started playing golf four years previously. On that day, I was the only player among them who scored lower than 100. I was so happy I bought dinner and drinks for them to celebrate. From then on, my golf has improved continuously. I scored 81 just five months after I first learned golf. That's when I went to the USA.

Because of my busy schedule in the USA I didn't think much about golf and didn't buy any golf clubs. Three months before I returned to Korea, I bought the latest golf clubs and played a round at a public golf club called Harding Park, in San Francisco. I made friends there with a man named John, a son of the Indonesian ambassador. He won the 2nd prize in the American Amateur Golf Competition. He handed down all his techniques to me as we played together in the afternoon every day for those two and a half months.

After I returned to Korea, my score has always been maintained in the 70's. I was crazy about golf and practiced a lot. I played with club champions once a month with such greed for victory and tenseness, that I even anticipated my fellow players' errors. I couldn't really enjoy golf and eventually lost sight of the purpose of golf. Despite this I was very successful as an amateur golfer with three 60's, 27 eagles, three triple birdies, and par plays for 18 holes.

In September 1998, I was hit by a drunk driver on the way to my office in the morning. I was hospitalized for two months with a ruptured cervical spine ligament, damaged nerves, and disks. I had to stop playing golf for a year. Although I had liked golf so much, I didn't want to play golf anymore. I had a good opportunity to think about golf again. Looking back, I realized that I hadn't enjoyed golf at all. I was just a slave to golf. Now, I have completely changed my views on golf. I enjoy nature and relieve my stress by playing golf only with friends, family, and colleagues. I abide by the rules, I do my best in my shots, and have a good time playing. I play a nice game and enjoy myself. In golf, you have to walk together with and always consider, your companions. That is why it is called the sport for gentlemen.

In the past, I was always excluded from betting when playing with fellow professors at my hospital. However, now I adjust my play inconspicuously to concede to, and have a good time with, them. I am glad when I target a bunker with my second shot and the ball falls in the bunker. The other players are also pleased when my ball falls in a bunker! In fact, this is the reason that my bunker shots have improved lately!

My fellow amateur golfers, I hope you will become a true amateur golfer who considers his opponents and enjoys the game.

15. Other Tips about Golf

1) It often happens in golf that misfortune turns into blessing. Therefore, you should not be concerned with your missed shots too much. Make every shot with prudence and a positive mind.

2) There is always an element of antinomy in golf. Do not try to conceive psychological factors before playing a shot. Make a shot comfortably and as you have practiced.

3) Before praising another player's shot, watch him carefully to try to learn from him, and try to imitate his swing.

4) Many golfers mistakenly think that the tee shot is the most important. In fact, it is the opposite. The putt is the most important shot in golf. Become a master of the short shot.

5) There are general and detailed theories in golf. Examples of detailed theories are: watch the ball, raise your arms, and use your waist. The general theory is rhythm. Three S's are required for maintaining rhythm: Slow, Short, and Soft.

6) Golf is the most generous sport of all. It is designed in such a manner that even if you miss one shot on any hole, you still have a chance to make par. You need to cultivate the habit of forgetting missed shots and calmly concentrating on your next shot.

7) Golf is like married life. You must not be one-sided to be happy. Sometimes you

need to sacrifice yourself for others and overcome ordeals with endurance to achieve the desired results.

8) Golf is a game of time. Time not only for you but also for your team and other golfers. Many people spend too much time setting up, only adding tension in their muscles. You should move naturally as you practiced without any thought. Saving time is good for you and others.

9) Golf is like the long journey of our lives: we climb mountains and cross rivers with heavy burdens on our backs. Getting angry and upset at one Out of Bounds only makes you breathe faster. If your heart beats faster, your behavior will become hasty, and your golf will be ruined.

10) People complain about the relative difficulty of a green. Imagine a golf game without greens and putter shots. It would be as dry as dust. We should all be thankful about the difficulty of the green. We are all playing in the same conditions. If you complain, you will only get lost in a pitfall.

11) Amateur golfers are suffering from the illness of "If only." They think, "If only I had not made that Out of Bounds / lost the ball / three putts today!" Such thinking is silly because these things are already reflected in your handicap. You are an amateur golfer, and your colleagues love you because you make such missed shots often. It's the same reason that high school baseball is so popular.

12) There is a phrase that, "Pros regard golf as a mode of living, and amateurs regard golf as a mode of life." Pros play for the numbers 2, 3, and 4 (short, middle and long

holes), while amateurs seek the numbers 3, 4, and 5. It is the unique charm of golf to try to approach the numbers of pros. However, greed should be avoided. If you just play comfortably with the numbers 4, 5, and 6, your skills will improve before you know it.

13) Your positions are different between practice and actual play. Your attitude also changes. In the actual game, you only have one chance to make the shot.

14) Someone said that GOLF stands for Grass, Oxygen, Light, and Foot.

16. Korean Golf 'Manias'

By Nam Hwa Young / "Golf Digest" Korea Edition Reporter

There are some areas of a manias' world that are inaccessible to ordinary people. They exhibit an amazing concentration, give out most unexpected ideas, or link completely separate things with novel connections. Their life is focused, sometimes to superhuman levels.

When spring comes, special genes in the body of golfers wake up. Often displayed as a discharge of adrenaline. Other symptoms include an unusual sensibility for the color green, a sudden urge to make a putting motion while walking on the street, or an illusion of seeing driver shots while watching baseball players swing on TV.

Golf manias are possessed of sensitive feelings. They even have some people around them telling them that he or she is crazy, but they seldom care about it. They also display excellent powers of concentration, pleasant monotony, or witty ideas. While playing golf, they find the strength to overcome the difficulties of life, and experience dialectic sublimation that breaks down walls.

In USA, they have the 'Golf Nuts Society', which organizes general meetings and competitions every year, and awards "Golf Nuts of the Year." This mania culture is not popular in Korea yet, and there is no association of golf manias. Nevertheless, Korean manias' passion for golf is no less than that of American counterparts. I have witnessed many living examples and some of them are presented below.

Finding the will to live

Mr. Gwan Joong Park, an international trading businessman living in the Middle East, plays golf in the desert. He used to play golf in the midst of thunderstorms, but playing in a sand typhoon in a desert was by far the most difficult experience for him. On a Saudi desert golf course, when visibility was barely one meter, he managed to complete all 18 holes with the help of a motor cart. After each of these three rounds, sand kept coming out from his nose and ears for three days.

Often during midsummer days, he would start a tee shot at 4 in the morning and finish putting with the help of the headlight of his car since it was after sunset. His longest rounding record on a desert was 69 holes, all the while pulling his own cart. Once he rounded 54 holes in a desert devoid of even a tree when the highest temperature of the day was 52 degrees Celsius. All he ate all day was 3 cups of instant noodles. But, how did he obtain boiling water in a treeless desert?

In his living room, the carpet, which couldn't endure so much punishment, was replaced with an artificial mat designed for use in deserts. Even the curtains were mobilized as articles for his practice. His golf clubs follow him wherever he goes in his car all the year round, along with 2 pairs of shoes, for desert and for grass.

Like a raw ore turned to a precious stone, a serious traffic accident he experienced three years ago helped him be reborn as a golf mania. After the accident, his body was covered all over with wounds, and he went through 5 major operations, during which three fingers were amputated. As well as that, broken shoulder blades and kneecaps were treated, and one meter of colon was cut off owing to a rupture of the abdomen. However, he didn't give up golf. Rather, he felt the will to rehabilitate through golf, and he even thanked the accident for helping him find the true joy of golf.

Image Golf

Mr. Hyeong Sang Mook, CEO of an online trading company, is a golf doctor. He taught me many secrets of golf. I'm convinced that he knows every thing there is to know about golf. He even writes physical formulas on a white board to explain the relationships of trajectory paths, flying distances, and swing speeds. He has 7 drivers, 6 iron sets, and 80 putters.

His golf career spans 11 years. He became a single-handicap player in only one and a half years. His ability improved remarkably after he was appointed as a branch office manager in Silicon Valley USA and moved to a new house in a golf club. This allowed him the time to round 72 holes over the weekend.

Worthy of his "golf doctor" title, his training method is very unique and efficient. Instead of going to a practice field, he trains his lower body by walking up and down the stairs of his office building, and repeatedly practices 1.5m putting in his living room. Is that all? He answers: I practice imaginary golf in bed. I fall asleep at around hole no.9. The next night, I restart from hole no.10.

His hobby is to read golf books and research golf. He has read over 300 golf-related books, and subscribes to five domestic golf magazines, 4 English magazines, and 3 Japanese magazines. He sometimes contributes articles to golf magazines. His dream is to round every one of the world's top 100 golf courses. Tonight, as always, he will play imaginary golf before sleeping, and explore one of the world's top 100 courses in his dream. God bless him!

I Know Nothing But Golf

Professor Ho Il Yang who teaches applied art at a university paints a picture of every golf course he rounds. He says, "I carry a secret camera. When I see a nice scene, I draw it out and take a quick picture without anyone knowing it. I start to paint the picture as soon as I come back to my atelier after printing the photograph."

His research room is filled with some 80 oil paintings of golf courses. He plans to have an exhibition after it reaches 100 paintings. When someone praises a picture of his, saying, "I like this picture," he presents it to him/her and paints another picture the same.

Professor Yang's 24 hour day is exceptionally simple. He started to play golf about 20 years ago in order to recover his health after suffering from alcohol addiction. Since then, he has spent every weekday lecturing at the college in the morning, and weight-training in a fitness club in the afternoon, as well as exercising for strengthening of his left hand and lower body to improve his golf swing. After returning home utterly worn-out, he would drop off into a deep sleep before 9 pm, and wake up at 5 am next morning. It has become his habit for the last 20 years. He is a true golf mania who devotes all his life to golf.

King of Records

958 rounds in a 15 year golf career, 84.67 shots per game on average since the first rounding until present; Mr. Deok Sang Kim is a king of records. He has rounded about 200 golf courses in 20 countries including Rotorua golf course in New Zealand that has hazards from which lava pours out. Anyone who has rounded with him would pay a tribute to his thorough recording spirit.

Aside from basic data such as the number of roundings and dates for a year, he keeps records of every detail including average and cumulative shot counts, 3 putting counts, the percentage of fairway safe arrivals, the numbers of pars, bogeys and penalty shots, together with notes such as his opinion on his companions' abilities as well as who paid for what. His passion for details does not stop here. He even created his unique score card form to record the features of each hole, attacking know-hows, and mental attitudes. Furthermore, his score card is made in such a way as to easily analyze the flying distance and direction of the ball. Now many golf clubs give a yardage book that contains descriptions of the course, but he has personally prepared a pocket book titled "Stroke Saver" many years ago. After a hole-out, he gives evaluations of each companion's play based on detailed data in 18 subjects, from grips to mental attitudes, not to mention advice for improvement.

Korean golf manias have a few common features. They do not postpone golf appointments for anniversaries or national holidays. Their living rooms have clear marks of "a golfer's home." They recall every detail about the day's rounding. They know how someone played by just looking at the flying ball.

Invariably, they keep records about how and when they played, with whom and in which golf courses. Can we recognize these people at a glance? It's difficult for ordinary people to find golf manias. These golf nuts emanate an aura, but some of them try to hide it. We cannot find them by face or voice. If you happen to find one, stick to him like crazy. You will surely get something: a free lesson, a know-how for selecting clubs, or a mindset. What you learn will surpass the scope of your common sense.

17. Korean Woman Power in Golf

By Han Eun Goo / Golf Reporter , The Korea Economic Daily

The whole world is watching in amazement at the growth of Korean lady pro golfers. In each competition of the US LPGA tour, Korean golfers occupied almost all the top 10 positions. This success has drawn the attention of the press from around the world.

Why are lady pro golfers doing so well while their male counterparts are not?

The reasons become clear after visiting the competition venues. I visited the Orchards Golf Club in South Hadley, Massachusettes to cover the US Women's Open in July 2004. I could meet Korean players more easily than 2 or 3 years before, since there were more than 20 Korean players. The ratio was one Korean to every 7 or 8 other nationalities.

A unique thing about Korean players is that their fathers are invariably following them. This is known as "Golf Daddy." The fathers follow the every step of their daughters like shadows on practice greens and driving ranges, feverishly giving guidelines. They observe every slight motion of their daughters throughout the rounding; after the game, they encourage and give advice about unsatisfactory parts of the play.

As can be seen from this, Korean lady golfers' driving force is from the power of their fathers. The interest and passion of their fathers, who have practically shared their life since the players were young, have fostered world-class players despite the barren reality of Korean golf.

Mr. Joon Cheol Park, father of Seri Park, is the original "golf daddy." It is well known that he used to let Seri practice at night in a public cemetery to build her courage. Though Seri has a dedicated coach, Tom Creavy, her father still personally coaches Seri Park on details.

"Golf genius" Michelle Wei also was most influenced by her father, Byeong Wook Wei. The reason that she changed her dedicated caddie to her father during the US Women's Open was because it was her father who knows her the best. In an interview with Golf Digest, Michelle Wei revealed the secret of her explosive long distance shot, saying that it was the effects of goat soup and snake soup her parents prepared for her.

Like Michelle Wei's parents, Korean parents of golf players not only teach their children everything about golf, but also manage physical strength by giving various stamina foods, and devote everything to the success of their children.

In addition to the golf daddy's role, the players themselves also did their best to succeed. Korean players are regarded as "practice bugs" in the LPGA tour. It's the Korean players who appear the earliest and leave the latest on driving ranges. They show more patience and endurance than any other nationality. It is not an overstatement to say that in reality, they play golf for the success. In Korea, whenever Seri Pak, Grace Park and Mi Hyun Kim return home, TV and newspaper reporters throng around them. The players who receive this national support cannot but focus only on golf.

Furthermore, golf has made big money for Korean players. Seri Pak and Grace Park earn more than one million dollars as prize money each year. In addition, they accept huge sums of money for contracting with Korean companies, not to mention additional incentives according to their play results. In USA, women's golf is much less popular than men's and the prize money is low, but in Korea, it's the opposite. Every week the reports on lady golfers who compete for championship cover the top of the sports section, and when they finally win, it occupies the top on the front pages of every newspaper. Because of this, the companies do not mind giving several billion won to famous players for advertisements. Even Korean pro baseball and pro soccer players earn much less than Seri Pak, Grace Park, or Mihyun Kim.

In Korea, golf became a shortcut to success for women. Accordingly, now many junior players are working hard everyday, with sweat running down in backs, while dreaming of becoming the second Seri Pak, in order to achieve fame and wealth.

1. Getting the Ball Close to the Hole

In order to get the ball close to the hole you must learn to control the distance of the putt or chip. A simple way to control the distance is to swing your arms like the pendulum of a grandfather clock. Swing the club back and forth in one-second intervals just like the clock swings its pendulum back and forth. Think to yourself 'tick tock' and make your stroke as even as possible back and forth. No matter what the distance to the hole is next time you putt or chip think of a clock ticking and you will get the ball close to the hole every time.

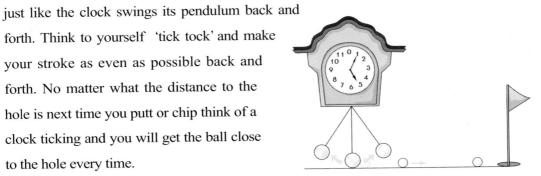

– Jason Kang

2. Roll the Ball on the Green

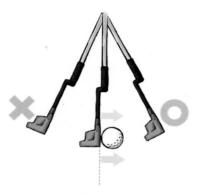

Rolling the ball is the key to making more successful putts on the green. When you hit the putt, meaning taking a short back stroke and accelerating forward, the ball tend to jump off the face and bounce along the green. When the ball hops you loose control of the speed and direction of the ball. The key to rolling the ball is to be as smooth as possible with your putting stroke. Take your backswing a little longer than you are used to and feel like your pushing the ball with your putter on the green. By pushing the ball, the ball will start to roll on the green quickly, which will help you make more putts.

– Jason Kang

3. Making a Divot

When you watch the pros on TV you see them taking a nice chunk of grass after each shot. This is known as a divot. Most amateurs try to hard to produce a divot instead of naturally allowing the swing to create it. Let me tell you a little secret. The divot is produced naturally, not forced. The divot should occur in front of the ball because Newton's Law of physics states, for every action there is an opposite and equal reaction. A divot is

created by the loft of the club, so a sand wedge will produce divot where as a 3 iron will not. So just remember don't try to make the divot let the swing and the club make the divot for you.

– Jason Kang

4. Reason Why You Top the Golf Ball

One of the major reasons why amateurs tend to top the ball is because they try to use their muscles to hit the ball instead of swinging the golf club. When you use your muscles to hit the ball, your muscles tend to contract towards your body thus making your golf club come short of reaching the bottom of the arc and hitting the top of the golf ball. Next time your playing imagine your arms as if they are ropes and allow the weight of the club swing for you arms. By allowing your arms to swing you will not only gain more yards, you will hit the ball more accurately.

– Jason Kang

5. Why do I Hit Behind the Ball?

One of the major reasons you hit behind the ball is because you don't transfer your weight properly. This means if you're a right-handed player you leave 90% or more of your mass on the right foot instead of the left when you have finished your swing. By not transferring you weight to the left you are causing the center of the arc to shift over to the right thus causing you to hit behind the ball. In order to correct this you must learn to stand on the left with the right foot barely touching the ground and hit the ball in this manor. This will give you a good feeling of what a good weight shift is and will help eliminate hitting the ball flat.

– Jason Kang

6. Hitting out of the Rough

Here is a little tip on how to get out of the rough. If the grass is so thick and you can barely see the ball, use the sand wedge and hit the ball back into the fairway. If you can see the ball in the rough this usually means the ball is sitting up so you can go for the green. In deep rough you must learn to swing the club as if the ball was sitting on a tee, not trying to force the ball out with brute strength. Many amateurs have a hard time hitting out of the rough because they feel that the ball will not go, so they try to muscle it out and by doing that their club slides underneath the ball not making sold contact. So next time your in the rough check out the lie and imagine you are hitting the ball off a tee for better results.

– Jason Kang

7. The First Shot

The first tee in golf is probably the hardest for any golfer so next time you are on the first tee try to remember this. First take two deep breaths, pick a target, and think slow and smooth. 99% of the time your tendency on the first tee is to get the shot over with as quick as possible. By taking the two deep breathes will slow you down a bit and help you relax. Next, pick a small target and forget your surroundings. Finally, make your back swing slow and smooth. This will help you find the rhythm of your swing.

– Jason Kang

8. Hazardous Bunkers

Hitting out of a bunker is easier than you think. Here are a couple of tips that you can use next time your in the bunker. Stand slightly open to your target, meaning align yourself just slightly left of the target. Open the club face slightly so that the club looks as if you added loft to the club. Then place the ball off to your left heal. Then twist your feet into the ground so you do not slip when you swing. Finally, make your swing all the way to the finish position and don't stop the swing just shortly after impact. Do not think you have to hit the sand exactly 2~3 inches behind the ball, just think you have to get to the finish position no matter what. So next time your in a bunker think 'ball off left heel' and finish the swing.

– Jason Kang

9. Concentrate for 10 to 20 Seconds

Many people say that golf is a game of concentration. If you play out of bounds (OB) or make an error, your powers of concentration immediately drop. Once you have played a triple bogey your mind goes blank. When this happens, your head is full of anger and confusion, not to mention losing your concentration. Under these circumstances, you can recover your composure only after three or four holes, or after you have played a good shot.

If you can routinely concentrate for 10 to 20 seconds before making a shot, it will greatly help improve your play. You should make it a habit to think only about and concentrate on this one shot. If your swing tends to hit the ball correctly, you will play the game calmly and carefully, shot by shot. If your swing tends to miss the ball, you feel bad and play the game carelessly.

This is the time when you should think over and practice the habit of concentration. Make the decision to just take 10 to 20 seconds to think and concentrate so that you can play the game well. If you try to concentrate, you will be able to enjoy golf better.

Two players who are famous for their powers of concentration are Jack Nicklaus and Annika Sorenstam, the queen of golf. There is an anecdote about Jack Nicklaus. Once, a player shooting before him made a hole-in-one, and people in the crowd cheered very loudly. However, he later said that he couldn't hear the sound. This story shows how much he concentrates on his game. Annika Sorenstam dislikes talking with her companions and seldom speaks during a round in order to concentrate on her game.

For amateur golfers, it is important to enjoy golf for friendship and have interesting conversations, but I hope we can concentrate on each shot, if only for 10 to 20 seconds.

10. Irregular Breathing Spoils Your Swing

One principle that I want to reveal for the first time is the breathing method. If you want to show off your swing, or if you become tense so as to play better, your breathing changes from its normal rhythm, and this is one of the causes of bad play.

Even if you don't intend to, your swing gets faster, and even if you don't intend to watch the flight path of the ball too soon, your head rises up. Lifting your head is not a cause, but a result of bad play. If your breathing is unstable and your body stiffens, a tension-releasing motion takes priority as a reaction, and you cannot move your body in the way that you wish. Getting agitated in anger, being out of breath after climbing a hill, feeling excited⋯ all of these cause irregular breathing and will spoil your swing. When this happens, you should calm your mind and control your breath, so that you take longer, more even breaths.

Breathing evenly is the only way you can make the same swing every time.

11. Golf Must be Natural

When a photographer tells you "Smile! You should smile to get a good picture," but it is difficult to smile and just feel awkward. However, if you are pleased, you naturally smile, even if someone else tells you not to smile. Just like your smile must be natural rather than forced, your golf must be natural as well. You can have the best grip, stance, address, swing, and finish by being natural and comfortable. This comfortableness, simplicity, and naturalness will make your golf game enjoyable. Your mind also should be comfortable, fearless, confident, and natural without being over-confident or over-comfortable. Always being natural and comfortable will greatly help you play better golf. This naturalness comes from ceaseless practice, and easy mind control comes from experience. I hope all of you will enjoy playing with a gently disciplined mind.

12. Just Hit the Ball

Golf is both easy and difficult. If you think it easy, it is easy; if you think it difficult, it is difficult.

Something that is easy on the driving range can be difficult in the field. This is not an easy problem to solve, but there is nothing that is impossible if you make an effort on a few points. "Just strike the ball" is what your right brain tells you. Worrying about your body functions and the OB to the right or hazards is the action of your left-brain. Thinking too much during a shot paralyzes your right brain, and you cannot play well. In the field, you should not think much, but just look down at the ball and strike it. Also, remind yourself that you should not strike too low on the ball causing it to fly straight up.

Second, strike the ball as if you are practicing, without thinking. If you are too focused and every muscle of your body is tense, your swing will be poor as a matter of course. To release tension is to loosen your muscles and play like you are just practicing. In order to achieve this, you should get rid of your desire to play well. So, don't say that it is impossible to empty your mind, just play like you are practicing. Don't think about how you will make your swing, but just look down at the ball and strike it. On the driving range, on the other hand, you should brace yourself up and play as if it is a real game, regardless of your body being tense or not. Then you will obtain the desired results.

無心

Just HIT IT! It's just white ball

13. Solving the Problem of Shank

After a nice drive, you want to lightly fly the ball for your second shot. However, you hit a shank. Every one who has experienced this will know how it feels. What is "shank" in a word? Shank is when the ball does not hit the center of the face of club head, but the neck connecting the head and the shaft. When this happens, you should analyze the reason.

You have aimed at the center of the club head during your address and back swing, but you have lost your aim during your down swing. In other words, the problem is that the ball does not hit the center of the club head at the moment of impact, but the hosel of the shaft, even though you were aiming for the center of the club head. This means that your swing path became too extended in the front. Now, we just have to find what caused your swing path to break away.

There can be several reasons, but the most frequent one is when the wrists are released too early while moving from the outside in. This widens the distance between the arms and the body, moving the address position away from the originally intended position. The second cause of shank is when the club is opened, and its shaft hosel hits the ball before it is released fully. Of cause, the causes of shank can be analyzed in more detail, but it can be simply a result of a change of posture before returning to the original address position.

So, how can we cure these problems? The answer is simple. A professional golfer once taught me that I can solve this problem by putting two balls on the ground, with one at a distance of 8 to 10 cm front of the other, and practice addressing and hitting the front ball. Another effective exercise for curing shank is to erect a wooden plate or another obstacle in front of the ball and practice making shots without touching the obstacle. This practice trains you to make a correct swing path. If your club always moves along the correct path, your shank will be cured. However, you don't have time to practice in the field. Unfortunately, often once you make a shank shot, you will make them repeatedly.

For me, I use a secret method for preventing a second shank shot. When I hit a shank, I address with the end of the club head for the next shot, and try to hit the ball with the end of the club head. This is an instant prescription for shank. You can try this yourself and see how it works.

14. The Problem of the Occasional Golfer

Amateur golfers usually only get to play a round of golf once in a while. In this case, there is one thing that we should be careful of: our swing becomes faster. If our swing gets faster, our club comes down immediately from the top of the swing, and we end up swinging with our arms only, without using our body.
As a result our arms get tense, our head moves up, and we hit the top of the ball (topping). When playing a round after a long time, we should try to swing slowly.

15. Stance in the Field

The easiest way to take a good stance in the field is to find a point in front of the ball in line with the target, put your club head perpendicular to the line connecting this point and your ball, and take a stance parallel to this imaginary line. To check whether the stance is parallel or whether you have addressed the target accurately, you can try a half-swing follow-through to the target to see if your club is pointing toward the target. In other words, you are making an imaginary follow-through line and checking your swing path by making a blank swing. Similarly, you can check whether your swing follow-through will point to your target on an uphill or downhill, by taking a stance and stretching your club to the target. As explained above, to stand perpendicular to the target is to find a point about 1 meter in front of the ball and stand perpendicular to the line connecting the point and the ball. Another method is to line up your shoulders in such a way that you're left shoulder will point at the target. I hope that this advice will help you enjoy your golf game.

Part 18.

AMATEUR COLUMNS

1. How to Watch the Swing

A few days ago, I debated the issue of whether or not the front sole of the left foot should be raised and the weight subsequently shifted to the heel in follow through.

It is not easy for an amateur to learn something just by watching. Even when you watch a professional's swing, it is not easy to recognize the key points. When you hear, "Watch the ball carefully," you watch the ball, not a point on the ball. Similarly, when you see a pro's swing on video, you are watching the entire swing, not specific points.

However, we should try to look for details. For example, with the issue of whether or not to raise the sole of your left foot during follow through, you can see clearly whether the weight remains in the front or heel of the foot by watching a professional player's foot during their swing. We need to watch carefully the key points when we review a pro's swing, so that we can learn from them effectively.

As we have to know what to practice when practicing, it is also important to know what to look for when we watch. Amateurs should closely observe the details in a swing. It will help them greatly to improve their skills.

2. There is No Referee in Golf

There is no referee in golf. Every player notes his or her own score, and plays by the rules. They should refrain from cheating themselves or violating the code of etiquette. Everything is left to your own conscience. You are your own judge. That is one reason why golf is called the game for gentlemen.

Amateurs find it difficult when they have to play the ball as it lies on the fairway. Except for situations allowed for by the rules, you must play the ball as you find it. However, most people have touched the ball at some point in their career before they take the shot. An amateur player often touches the ball to move it to a better position. Don't be too stressed by rules, but you should try to play the ball without touching it. You will feel better if you follow your conscience. Everybody needs to make an effort to familiarize themselves with the sport for gentlemen, where there is no referee.

3. Characteristics of Single Digit - Handicap Players

Singles refer to one digit numbers or people who live alone. Every golfer wants a single score. Those who have scored a single score only once are considered single digit-handicap players. As well as those have scored many singles. That is the norm among amateurs.

All single digit-handicap golfers have been crazy about golf at least once in their life. They also have their own golfing philosophies. Professionals are different kinds of golf players than amateurs. There is something different about them. So too with single digit-handicap golfers. They all have their own strong points.

We know that golf is the sport of gentlemen. Single digit-handicap players should maintain a character on par with their capability in every respect of the game, including manners and rules.

Avoid fooling around too much, or giving unsolicited lessons while another player is addressing. Your actions should be worthy of your status.

4. Process or Results in the Game

There is a European proverb, "Pros value the process of the game, and amateurs value the result of the game." This applies to all sports, including golf.

The phrase suggests that professionals seek good results by placing emphasis on each and every shot. In contrast, amateurs are too attached to the results, so they miss the shot. In extreme cases, they insist that a ball that obviously landed in the Out of Bounds area is still alive, and change the ball's position. These are the results of placing too much emphasis on the result of the game, rather than a sincere desire to learn. We need to adopt attitudes of learning by making an effort to play shots under less-than-favorable situations. Your skills will not develop unless you cultivate the perseverance to overcome the bitterness of the dreaded Out of Bounds.

5. Golf Scores in Spring and Duff

Spring is a pleasant season. After a long wait in the cold winter, you can spread your wings and go outdoors again come springtime. As the ground frozen during winter thaws, the grass is dry, and it is very difficult to hit a golf ball. Often, in trying to hit the ball, you may end up hitting the ground.

At some golf clubs, it can seem like you are playing on a bare ground. Sometimes, when you swing at a ball sitting on what seems to be a healthy bed of grass, the ground underneath nothing but mud. Consequently, your club may get stuck in the ground and the ball will fall right before you. This is the greatest enemy of your score and your confidence.

These situations require skill. Do not release your wrists as you ordinarily do. Hold them longer and hit through the ball, as if striking at the ball. Select a one-or two-step longer club than usual, and take more care.

One thing to take note of is that your wrists play the most important role here. You need to release the wrists after the club pushes the ball through. If your wrists are released too early, you will not avoid a duff shot. It is not easy to score well in the early spring. As you are intent on hitting the ball, you may fail in adjusting for distance. Holes that were easy to par in summer are hard to par in spring. This results many bogies and double bogies

6. The Good Doer Is Rewarded By Heaven

In Myeongsimbogam (a classical Korean textbook), there is the saying, "heaven rewards good doers with blessings, and punishes wrong doers with disaster." I always feel that this also applies to golf.

When the ball is poorly positioned on the fairway, you may be tempted to move it slightly to a more convenient place before playing the shot. Try to resist this temptation. You will only disgrace yourself. Moreover, your efforts towards a poorly-situated ball may be better and more concentrated—making it a blessing in disguise. I only ever feel guilty when I touch the ball, especially if my subsequent shot is poor.

Every amateur feels the urge to touch the ball. Suppress this urge to win trust from your companions. Always remember the above saying, and try to become a well-mannered golfer who abides by the code of gentlemen.

> ★☆★ **Heaven rewards good doers with blessings, and punishes wrong doers with disaster.**
> This saying appears in the classic book called "Myeong Shim Bo Gam," and means that Heaven blesses someone who does well and someone who does not is punished by Heaven. With regard to golf, this saying urges us to become well-mannered golfers by observing the rules of golf.

7. The Threshold of a Single Digit-Handicap

Even if they train in a concentrated manner, amateurs always have problems. When it feels like you can hit the ball well, you may sprain your arm and need to rest for a month. Or, you may not have enough time to play golf because of a busy lifestyle. These obstacles will always follow one after another. The shortest period for amateurs to become single digit-handicap players is about one year. It is only attainable after correct and steady practice, and over 100 episodes of field experience over a year. Needless to say, you also need to take lessons.

Even after these efforts, a typical single score might be about 81, (nine over). Achieving a score in the 70's is more often than not impossible due to problems of the mind rather than technique.

In critical situations when you can score 79 if you play bogies for the last two holes, or if you make a par on the final hole, we will often ruin our game by playing doubles or O.B. because of the pressure to score in the 70's.

You can achieve scores in the 70's only if you have made the efforts mentioned above, if all of your driver, iron, approach, and putter shots are sound, and if you can control your mind to ignore the compulsion to score in the 70's. It is worth mentioning again that the most important things are the basics. You can never reap what you didn't sow.

8. Winter is the Season for Increasing Distance

You will go to the golf course less often in winter due to the cold weather and snow. However, you should not miss this opportunity to improve. This is the only opportunity for you to increase your distance. I took lessons for three months one winter, and I only practiced with a # 8 iron.

I then went to a golf course in the spring, and played a driver. To my surprise, the distance of my driver shot increased by 20 to 30 yards! My iron shots also sent the ball at least 10 yards further.

I learned from this experience that your distance depends on the amount of practice you undertake. Bear in mind that the less you practice, the shorter your distance becomes.

9. Single Digit-Handicap Players and Beginners Are No Different

Golf is fun. It is a characteristic of golf that players always try to teach lesser golfers how to improve, irrespective of the length of their own careers. Single digit-handicap players want to boast about their techniques, so they seek out companions who play worse than them.

On the flip side, beginners want to learn something from good golfers. Consequently, because they need each other, we can say they are in the same league.

Do not be proud of your good golf, and do not be ashamed of your poor golf. Professionals need the gallery, and the gallery needs the professionals to watch and learn from. Everyone is equal in golf.

Part 19.

PROFESSOR SUH'S ESSAYS: HEALTH AND GOLF

1. Play Two or Three Rounds Per Week

I once heard that a few years ago in Finland the government prescribed sports therapy for the health of their senior citizens. The senior citizens were advised to play a certain sport for a few hours every week. They complained that it was monotonous and uninteresting. The embarrassed Finnish government developed a new prescription: "Play golf twice a week, and walk the whole 18 holes." Since then, many senior citizens have recovered their health, the cost of healthcare to the state was reduced, and society was better off as a whole.

According to the report, it was revealed that after periodic rounds of golf two to three times a week, senior citizens' capacity for oxygen absorption improved greatly, the muscle strength and endurance of their waists developed, they lost weight, the fat layer around the abdomen thinned out, and their cholesterol levels fell. In other words, playing golf really is like killing the two birds of health and enjoyment, with one stone.

We often hear that exercise is good for seniors, but the risk of damage to muscles, bones, and the cardiovascular system accompanies every sport. However, it is known that golf has relatively fewer risks than other sports. It is non-contact. It is slow-paced. Make it a rule to play a round of golf twice a week. Your health will thank you for it.

2. Golf Elbow

In order to prevent golf elbow, adhere to the following rules:

Firstly, forget every piece of information about sports medicine that has since been found to be wrong, such as, "Pains gained from sports must be cured by sports."

Secondly, choose a good mat at the driving range. If the mat is worn out and the underside is exposed, the club head will touch the mat after your swing, and the impact will be directly conveyed to your arms.

Thirdly, check your golf clubs. Do not choose golf clubs based soley on the advice of others. Do not think that a certain brand of steel shaft will help you make a long-distance shot. Your clubs should be appropriate for your age and physical strength. If you are over 40, avoid steel shafts if possible, because it may burden your body too greatly.

Fourthly, be careful about chopping shots, especially if the grass is rough and the soil is hard. When you play chopping shots often, golf elbow can develop easily.

Finally, abandon your short temper. Do not try to become a single digit-handicap player in one day. It will only aggravate your long-term health if you try to cure your pain with a pain killing injection from a doctor.

If you take it easy and tell yourself, "I will just endure it for this round," your illness will only become worse. It may mean that you may not be able to play golf for a year. Golf elbow can also result in the need for surgery.

3. Prolotherapy

"I sprained my ankle." "My waist hurts. It must be a disk." "I caught golf elbow after I played too much golf." These symptoms are mostly caused by a lengthened or torn ligament or muscle.

In these cases, assessment by radiography is ineffective. When a bone is broken, you get a cast. But you have a sprain, the doctor prescribes a painkiller, and applies an elastic bandage. This therapy is not sufficient for the damaged ligament or muscle to recover completely.

One theory suggests that ligament or muscle damage cannot ever be completely eradicated. The theory suggests that ligaments and muscles cannot be restored to any more than 70% of their pre-injury condition.

However, there is a method to revive ligaments and muscles by injecting amplifier in the joints of ligaments and muscles. This method is called, "Prolotherapy." The injection formula uses a very safe drug that can be used in unlimited doses, unlike other muscle replenishing drugs like cortisone.

Prolotherapy is one of the best therapies around. It has shown satisfactory results, without relapse, in 80% of cases, even for chronic golf elbow.

4. Yips Disease

In 1997, the sports medicine center of the world—the renowned Mayo Clinic in Minnesota, USA—carried out an experiment with Yips. The experiment was led by doctors from the departments of rehabilitation, neurology, and endocrine. Many other experts from sports physiology, sports psychology, behavioral analysis, and physical therapy also participated.

The method of the experiment was to organize a putting competition—big money was at stake. 2,600 golfers with a 12 or lower handicap participated in this competition. 53% of them showed various symptoms of Yips disease, such as a stiffened body, trembling hands, stifling, and anxiety.

For the golfers to overcome this disease, Doctor Ainsley Smith, a professor of sports psychology at the Mayo Clinic, offered the following suggestions:

Firstly, practice steadily, without overexertion.

Secondly, learn to relax the muscles.

To do this, inhale deeply for 10 seconds, and then slowly exhale. While inhaling again, stretch your legs, and bring your ankles to your bust as far as they can go, until you feel the calf tighten. Hold for 10 seconds and then slowly exhale.

Thirdly, mobilize your imagination. Have confidence in doing it—whatever it is—correctly.

If you do not feel confident in the putting pose, step back, look at the lie again, and then set up once more.

5. Golfers in the Wounded Ward

As is the case with all sports, injury is the biggest enemy of golfers. Although golf is one of the safest sports to play, the probability of injury is higher than we might think.

There are many golfers who have had a difficult time due to unexpected injury on PGA tours. Tiger Woods was wounded in the waist and the Achilles tendon; Langer changed his putting grip due to lumbago; David Toms suffered from wrist pain; David Love III had to fight against injuries in the waist and neck for the whole 2001 season.

Many famous golfers suffer from muscle and skeletal pain. It is the same situation for Korean professionals. Every pro golfer I have met had one or two trouble spots in their body.

Some coaches demand absurd amounts of exercise and practice from their students because, "The one who practices more, wins." They often drive young golfers to injury with such unrealistic viewpoints.

One day, a junior golfer visited a hospital with a bended waist, and he said, "My coach requires me to hit 3,000 balls a day, so I had to practice day and night."

The two elements of rest and replenishment must be included in any scientific method of training. It is time to discard incorrect programs that consist only of training and competitions. We have to question ourselves if it is really right to practice golf with such unrestrained vigor.

6. An Unreasonable Swing Ruins Your Body

The muscles in our body naturally decrease by 1% a year from the age of 50. The elasticity of our muscles also degrades with age. This trend only accelerates the older we get. Our concentration also falls as our nerve tissue diminishes, and when we are over 50, the bundles of spinal nerves diminish by approximately 35%, and our response to stimulations declines by 10%.

Osteoporosis occurs because our bodies' ability to generate minerals in bones drops by 0.3 to 0.5% every year after the age of 30. Although it depends on the individual's diet, amount of exercise, and hormonal changes, it is known that bone tissue diminishes by about 30 to 40% by the time we become seniors. Our bodies' pliability also declines as our collagen's water content and elasticity falls. This means we are more susceptible to injury over time, and recovery takes longer.

One common factor among all these symptoms of aging is that they can be prevented or delayed with regular and appropriate exercise. Therefore, it is recommended for seniors to practice golf three to four times a week at a driving range, and play on a golf course on weekends. However, if you are not careful, and make unreasonably large swings, or take lessons without due consideration of your body's condition, you will only risk injury. Therefore, do not forget to warm up your body by stretching, and doing simple exercises before playing golf.

7. Women and Golf

Only a few years ago, you did not see many female golfers at the golf course on weekends in Korea. This has changed. The swing of female golfers looks more graceful than that of male golfers. However, when women practice as much as men do, the probability of damage to their muscles or skeleton system is higher, because most women have fewer opportunities to exercise.

Female golfers are particularly susceptible to injury in the elbows and wrists. The direct cause of this is a lack of muscle power and endurance in their upper bodies. Women also have weaker grasping power than men, which, combined with the weakness of their lower bodies, interferes with making a consistent swing. In addition, the greater pliability of women may be an obstacle in golf, because they cannot use the elastic power required for a powerful swing.

Therefore, female golfers must remember the following principles to improve their golf skills, whilst also preventing injuries. Firstly, they should invest more time in exercise, to build up muscle power in their upper body, including the arms and shoulders. Furthermore, they need to exercise crouching, stretching, and twisting their legs, to strengthen the key ligaments of the knees. If you are too pliable, and power is lacking in your swing, temporarily stop your pliability training, and place more emphasis on building muscle.

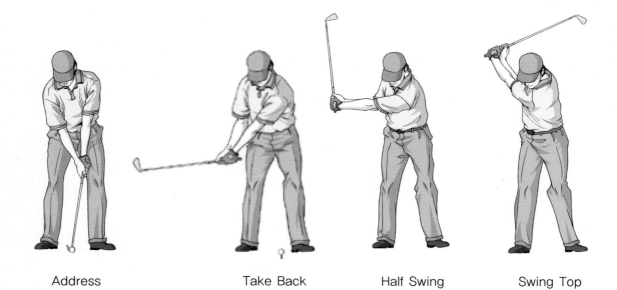

Address   Take Back   Half Swing   Swing Top

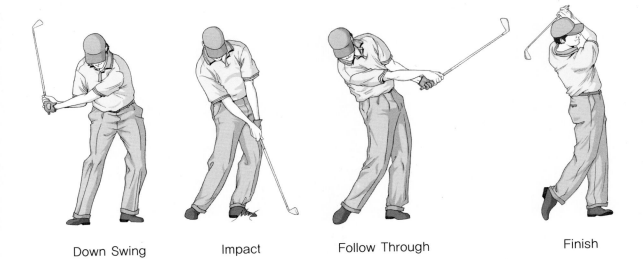

Down Swing   Impact   Follow Through   Finish